Butterfly
Coloring Book

I0491305

Aryla Publishing 2020

978-1-912675-81-4

www.arylapublishing.com

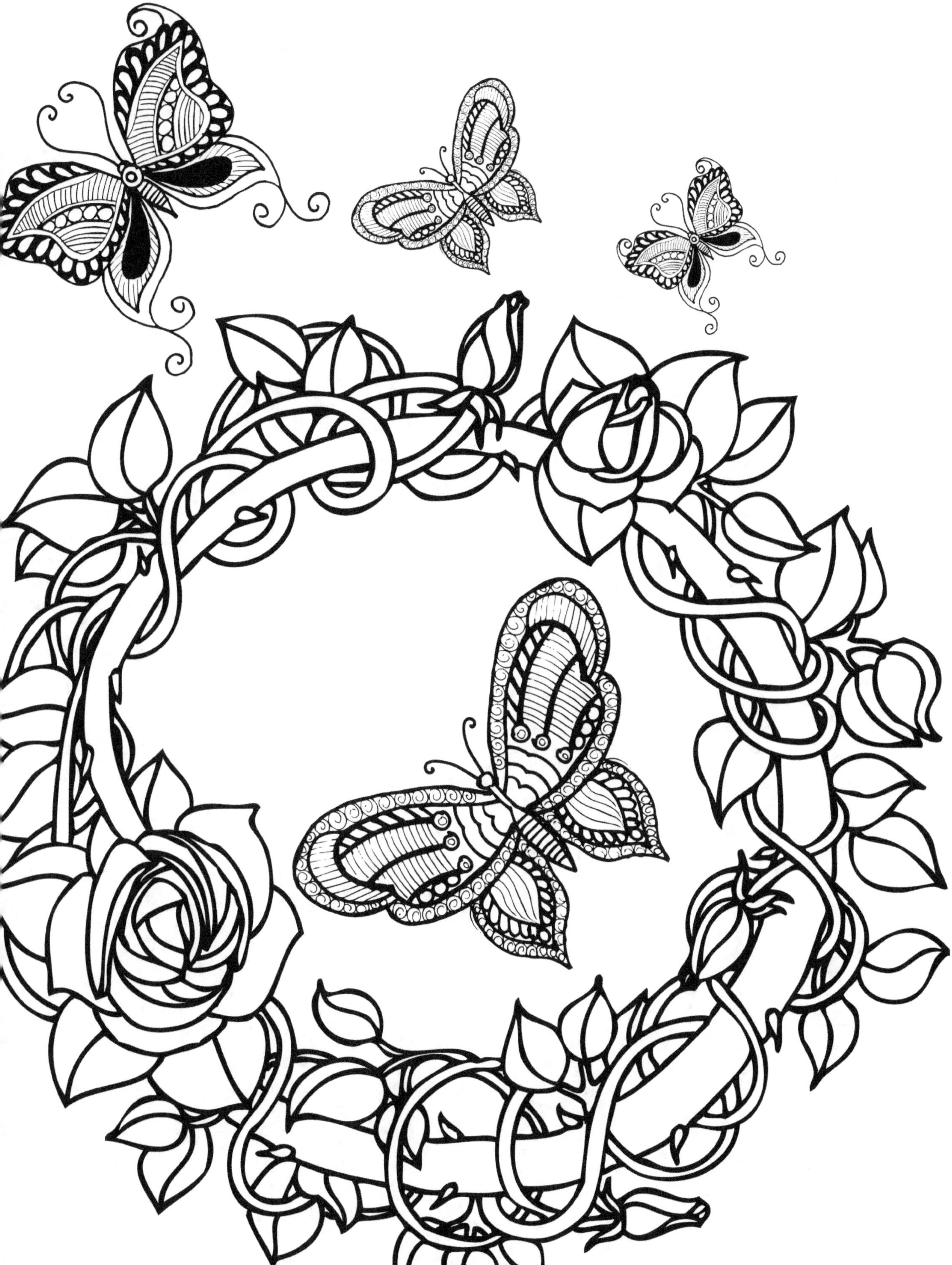

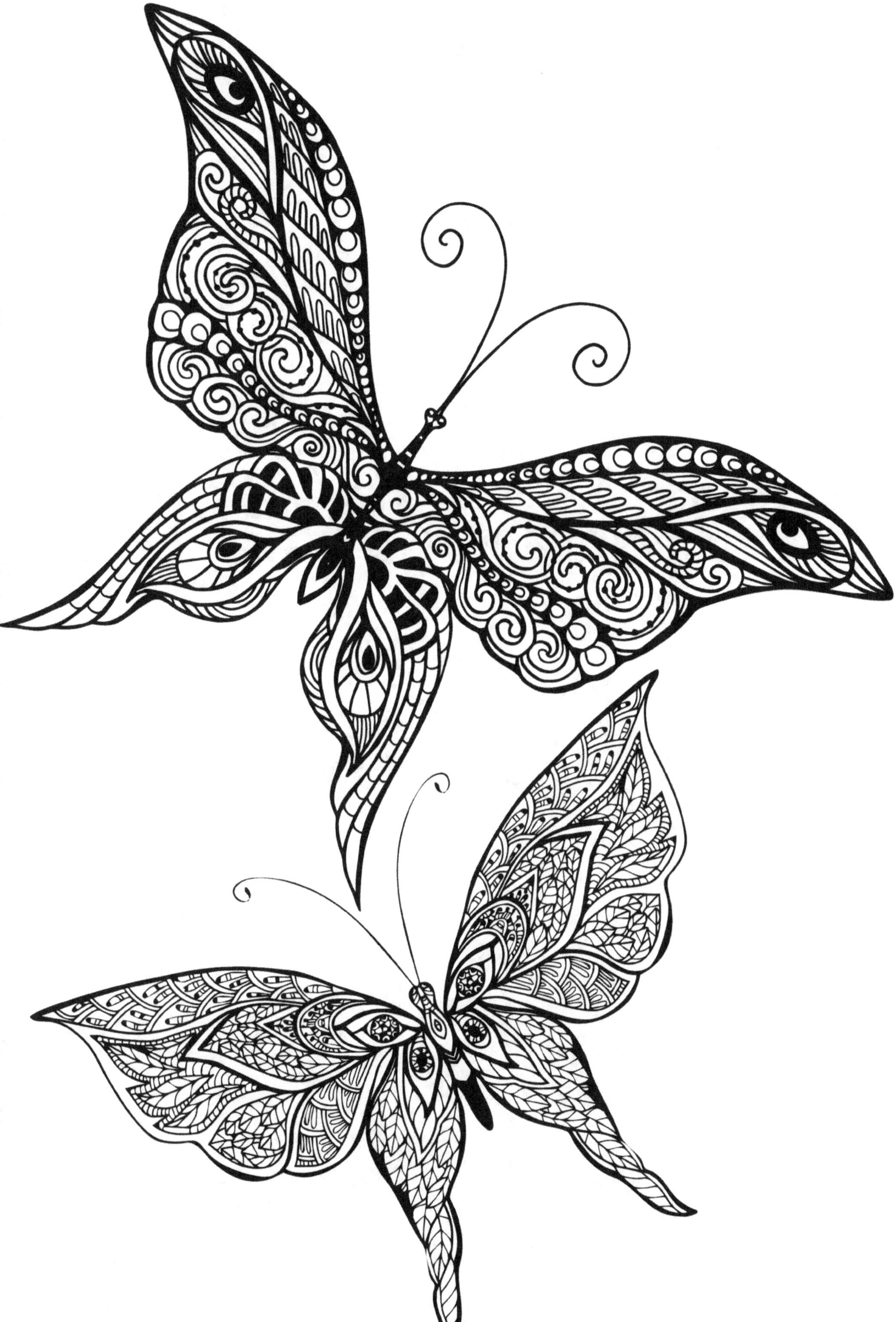

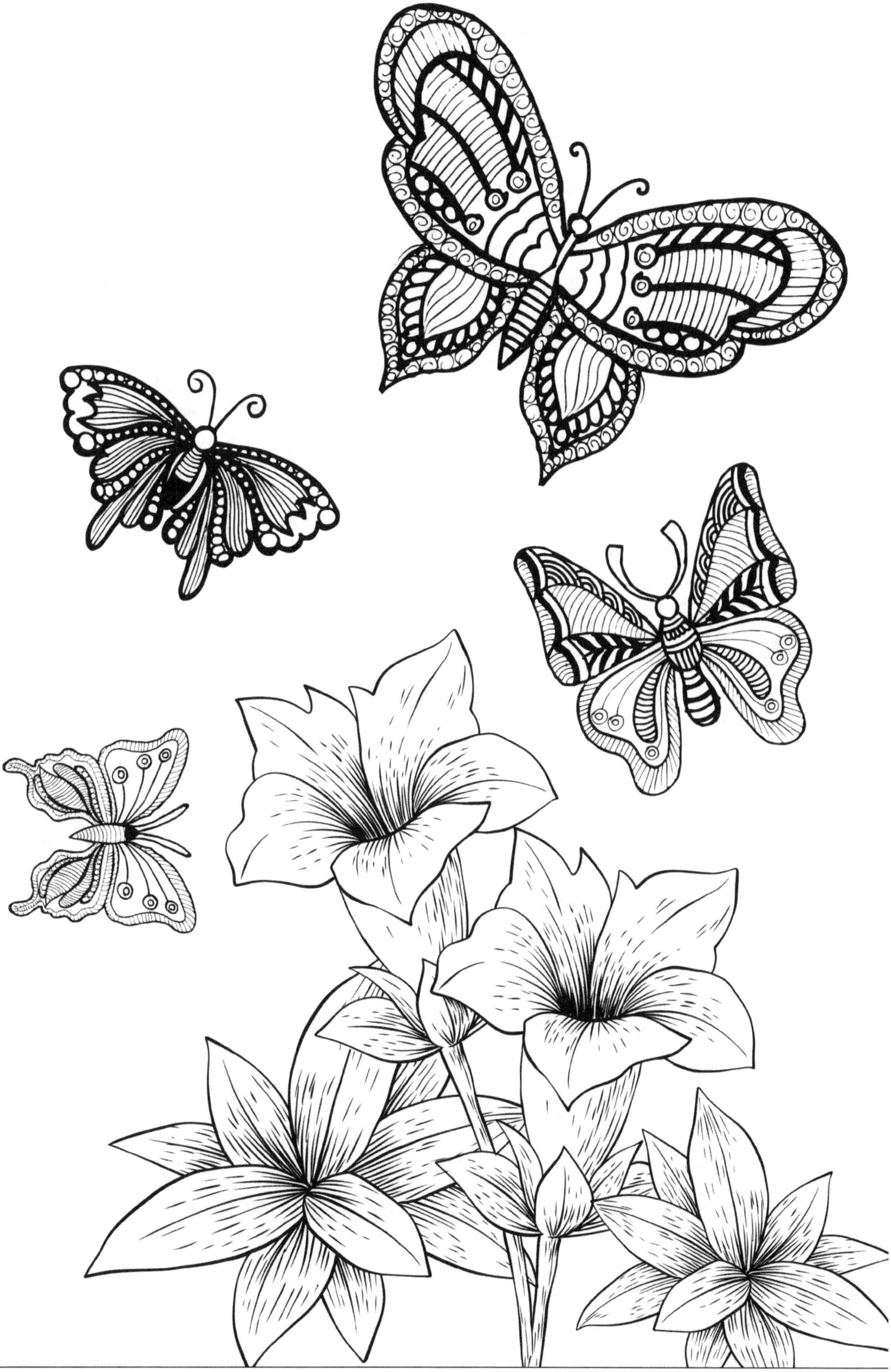

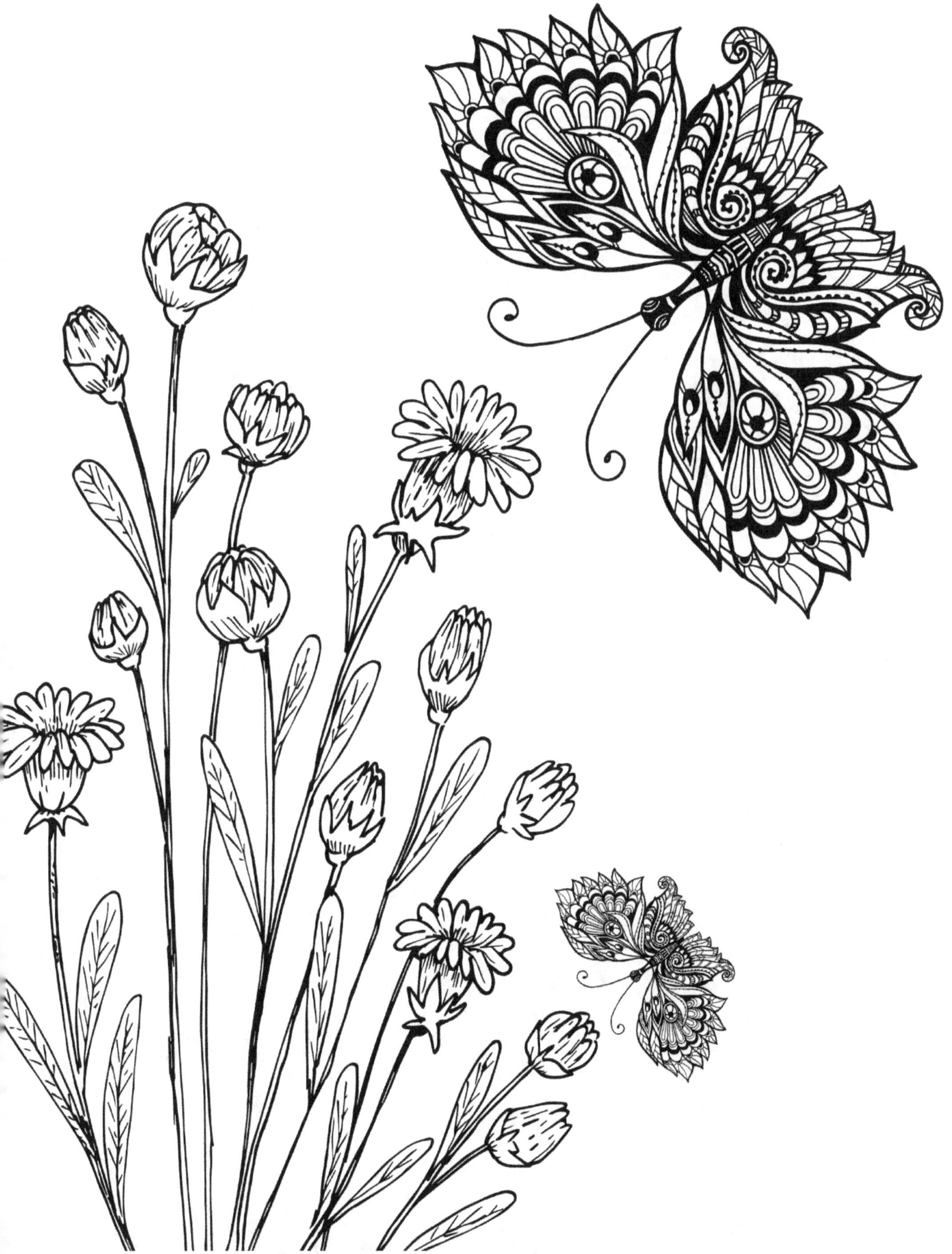

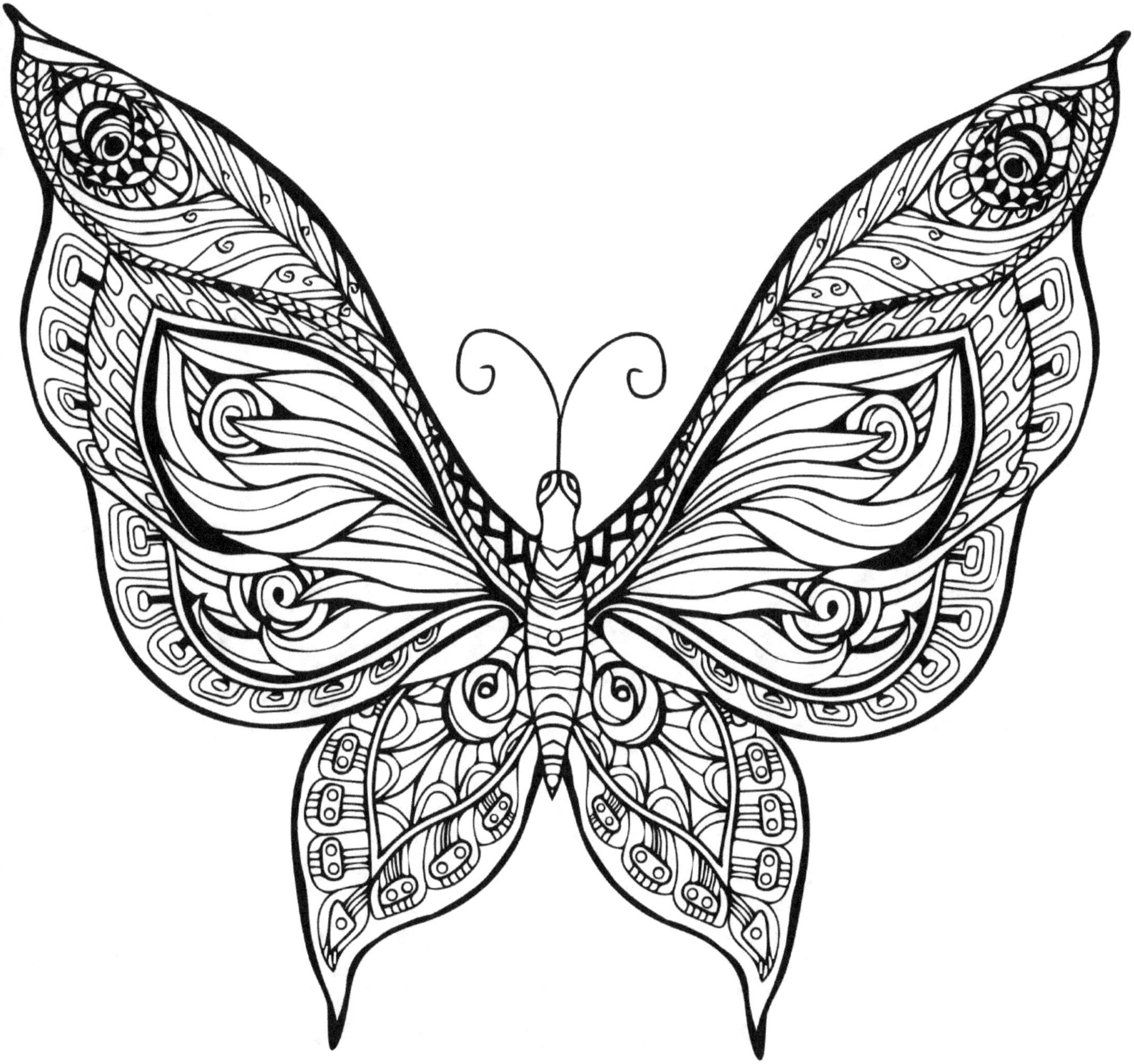

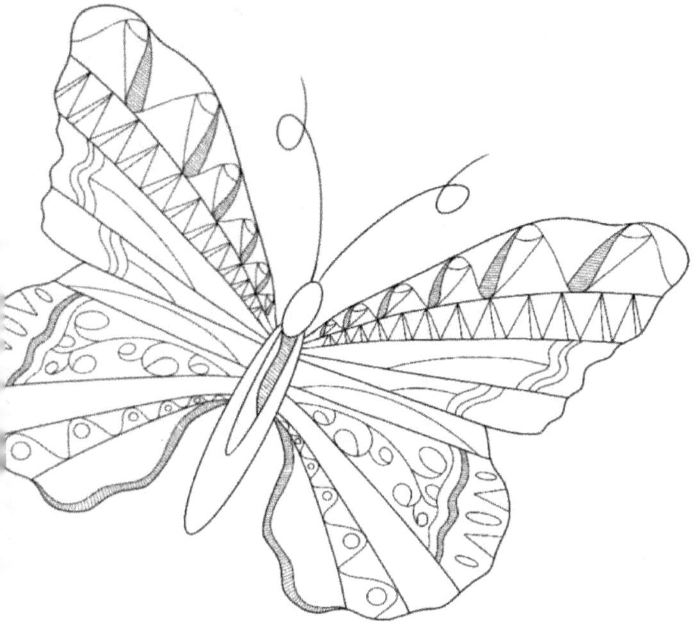

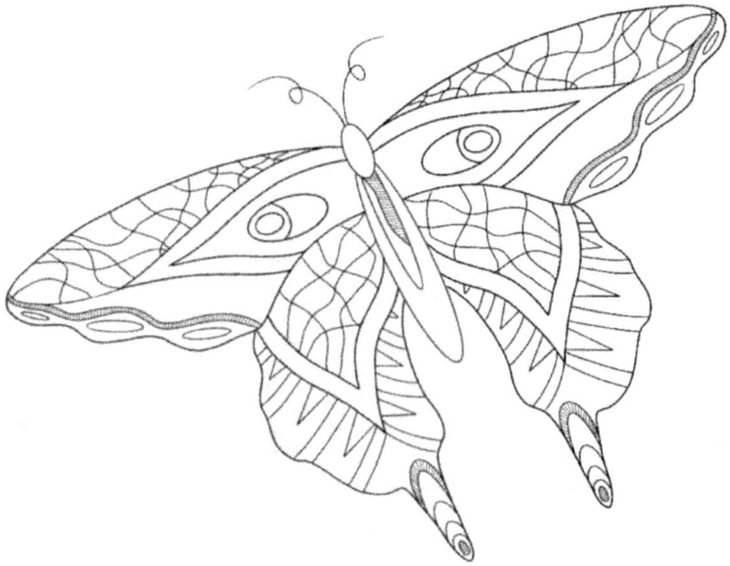

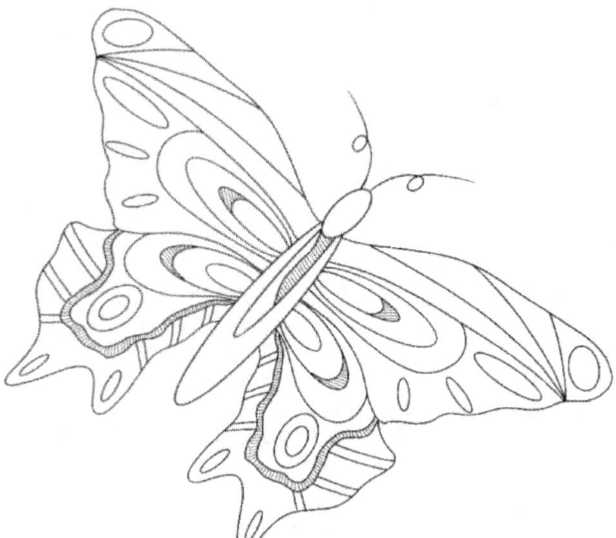

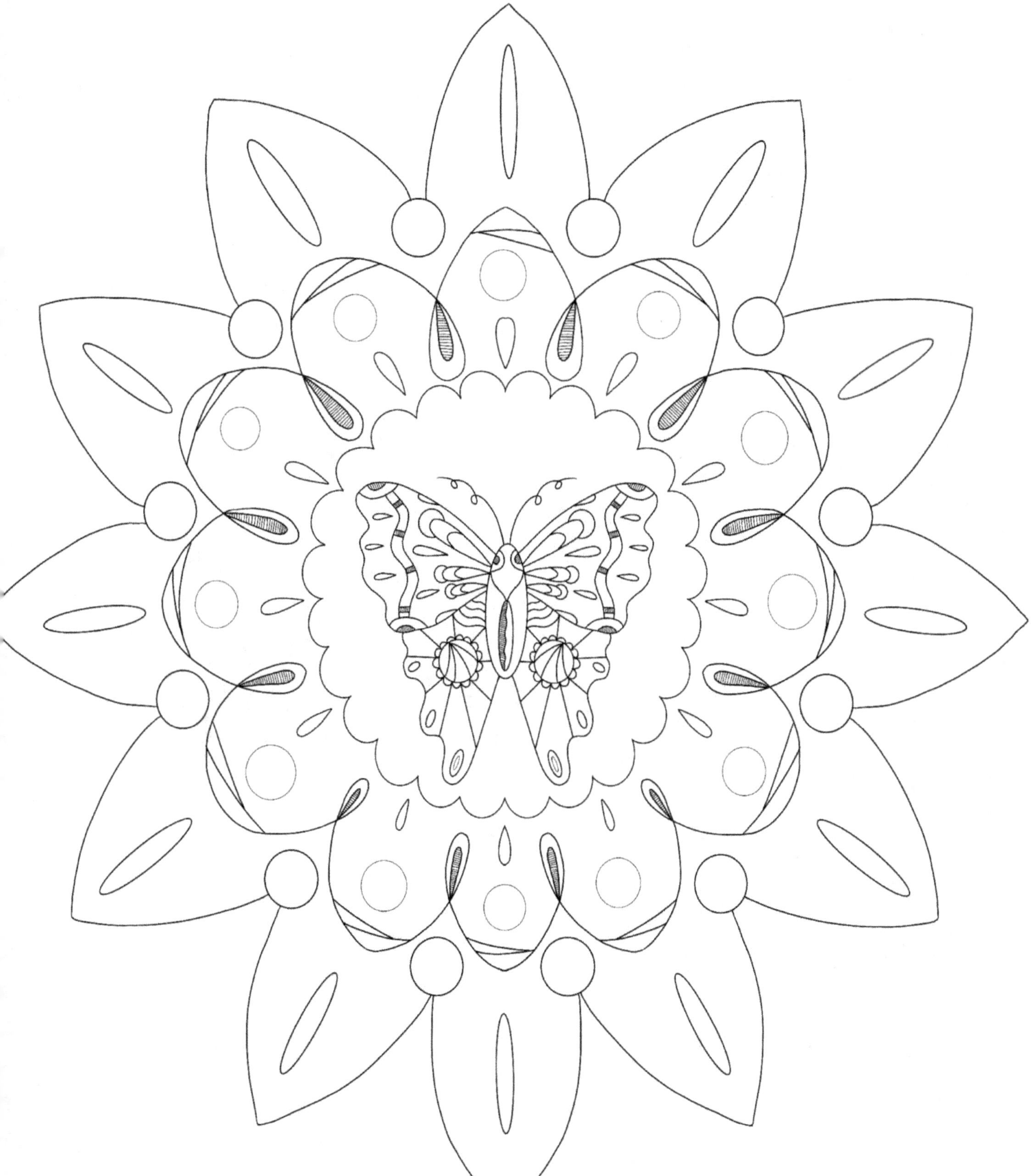

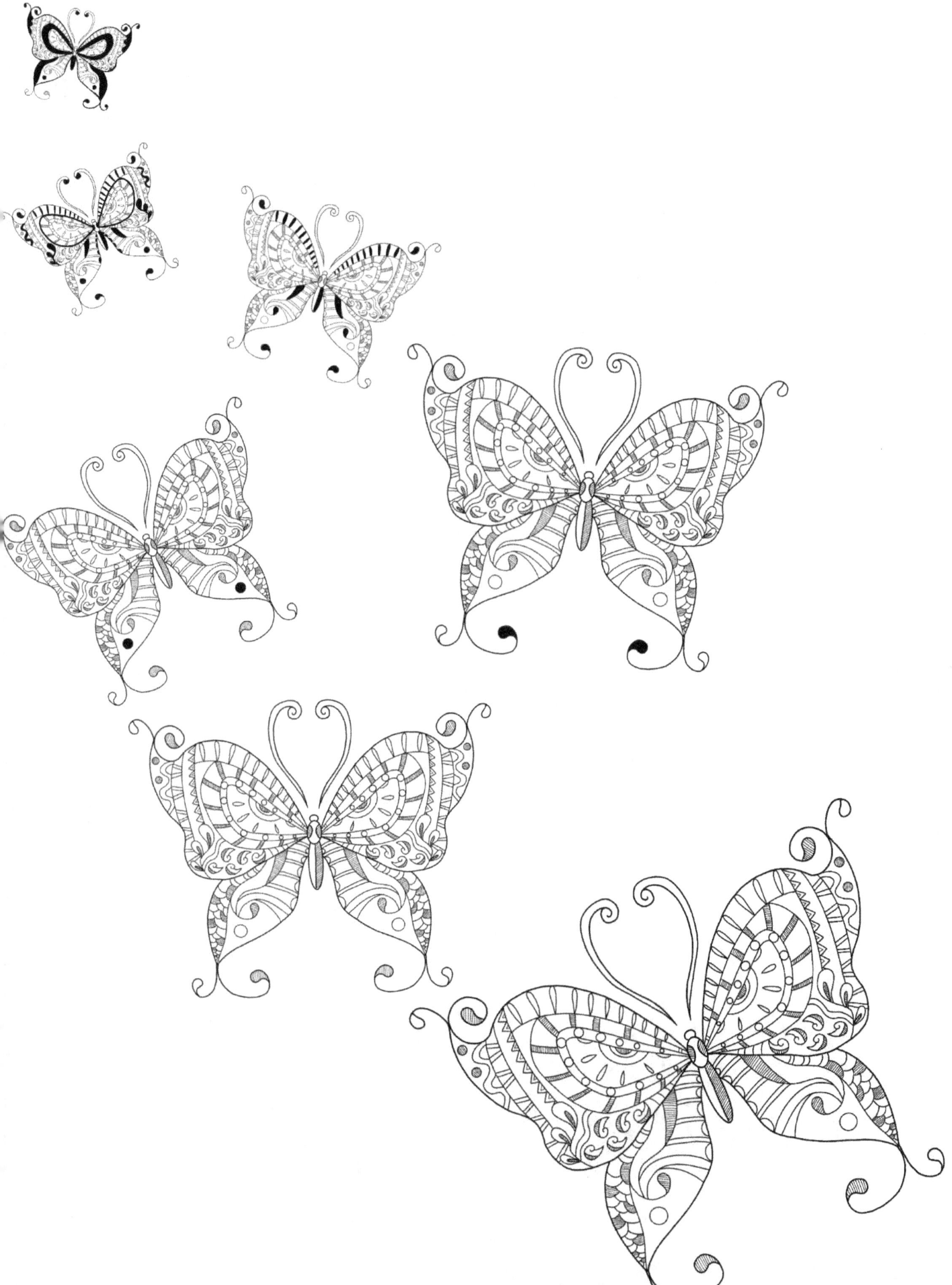

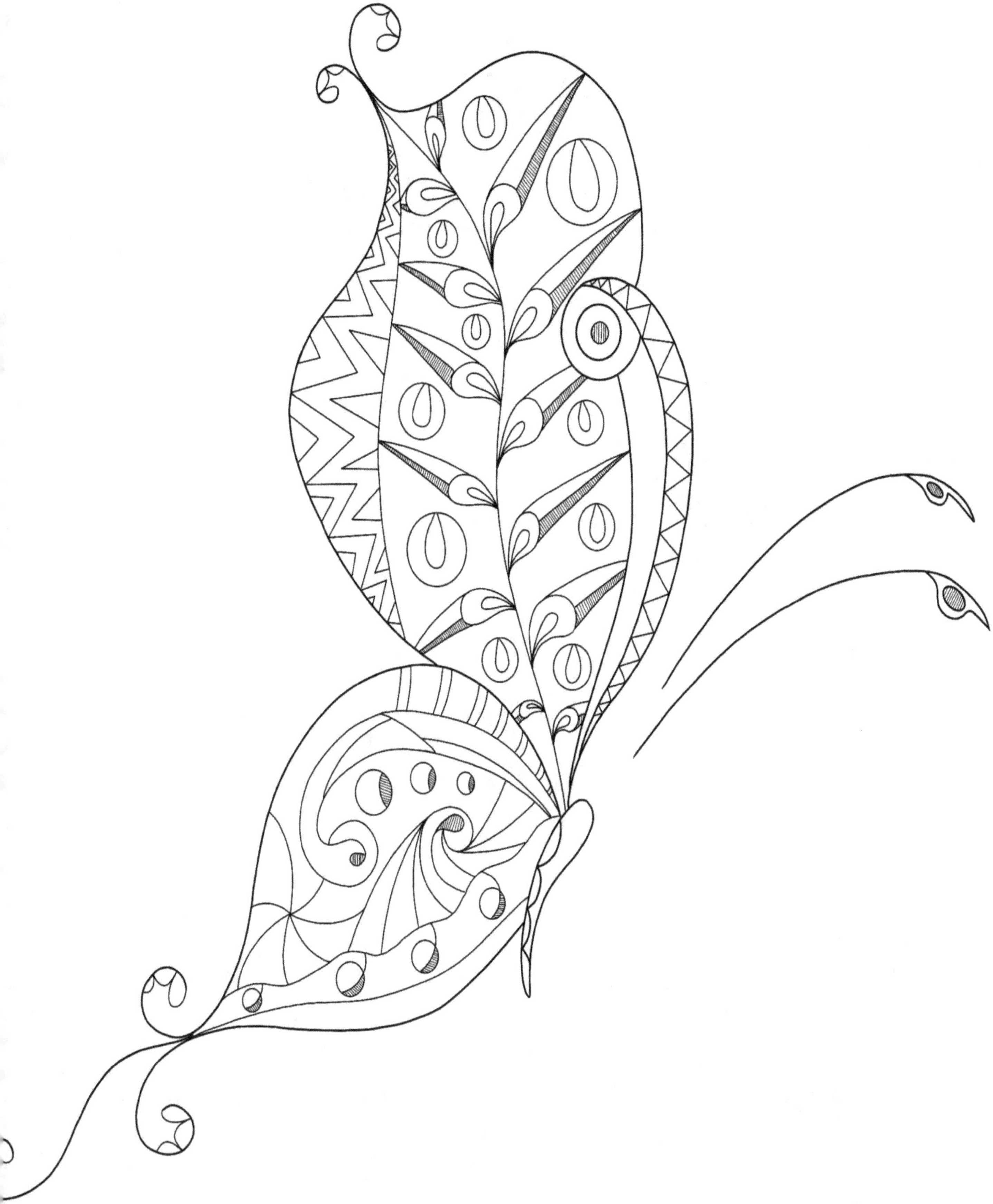

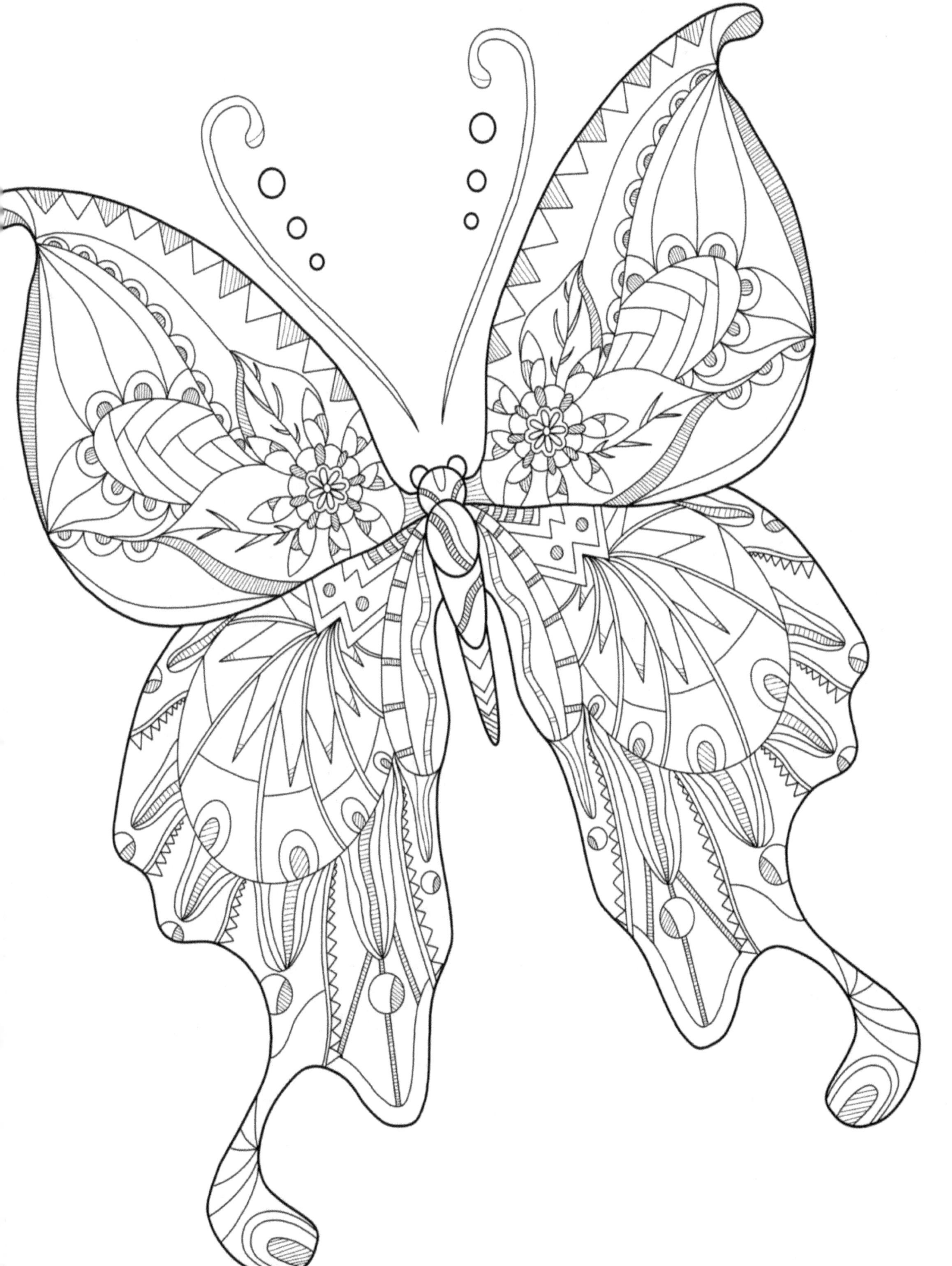

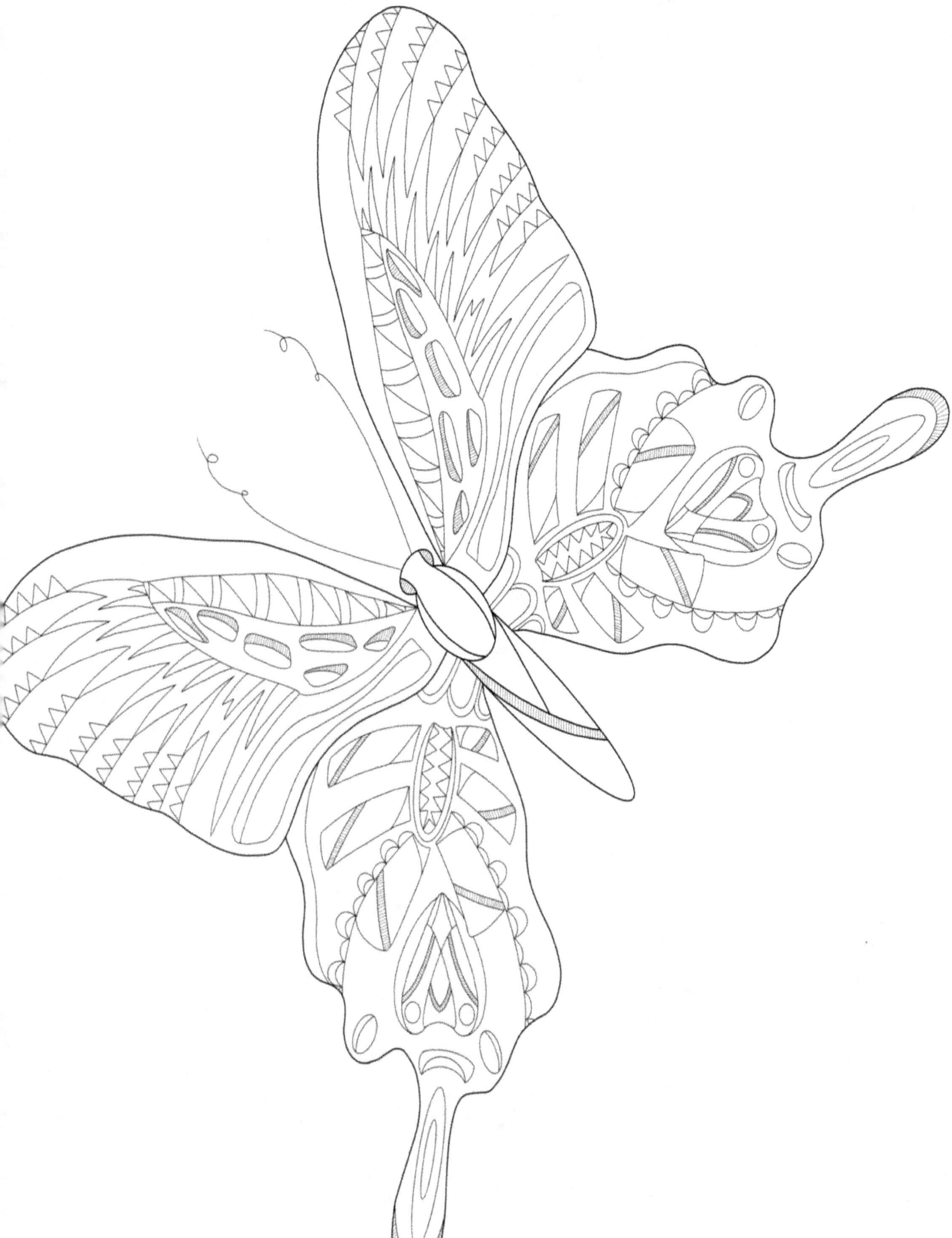

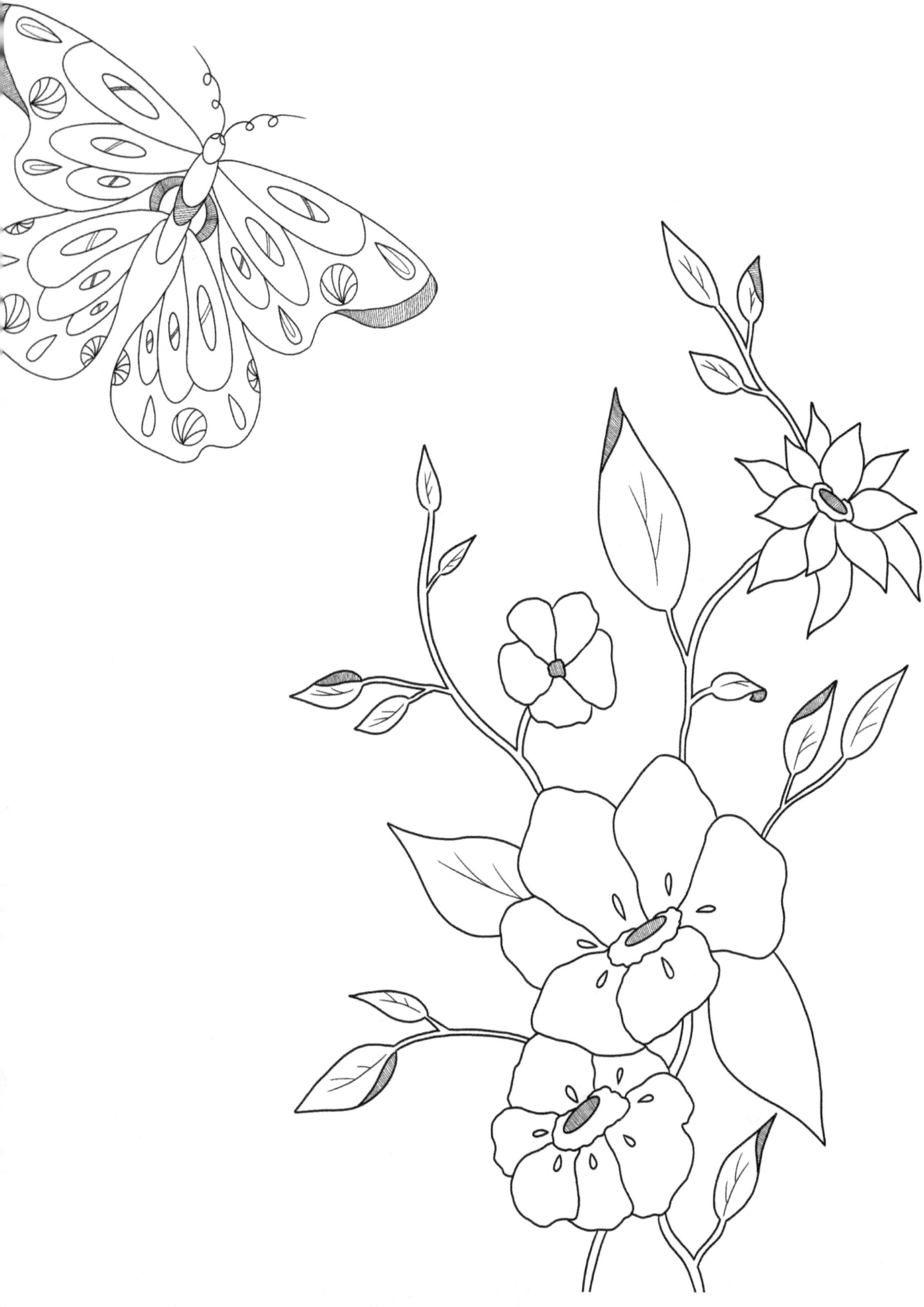

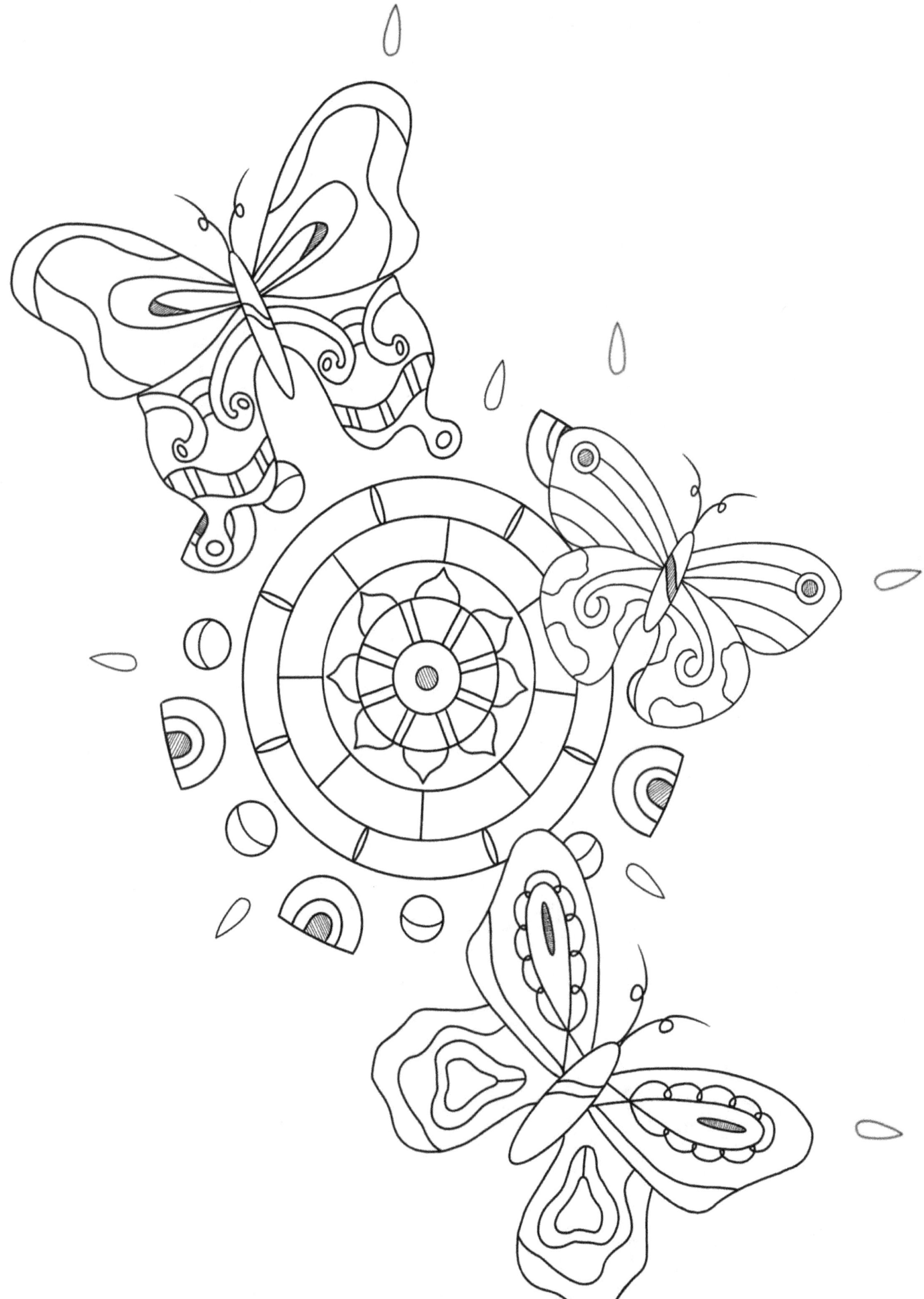

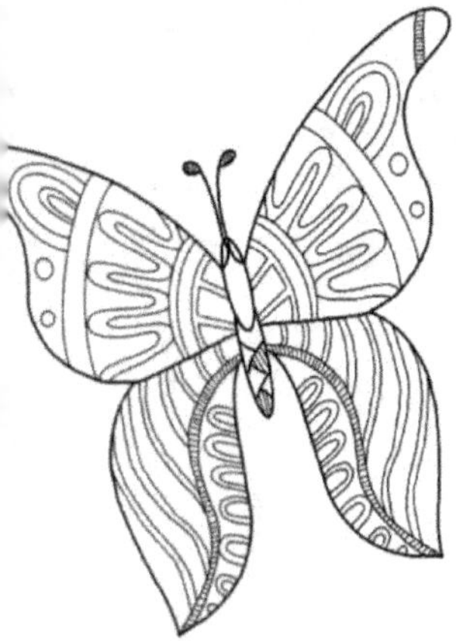
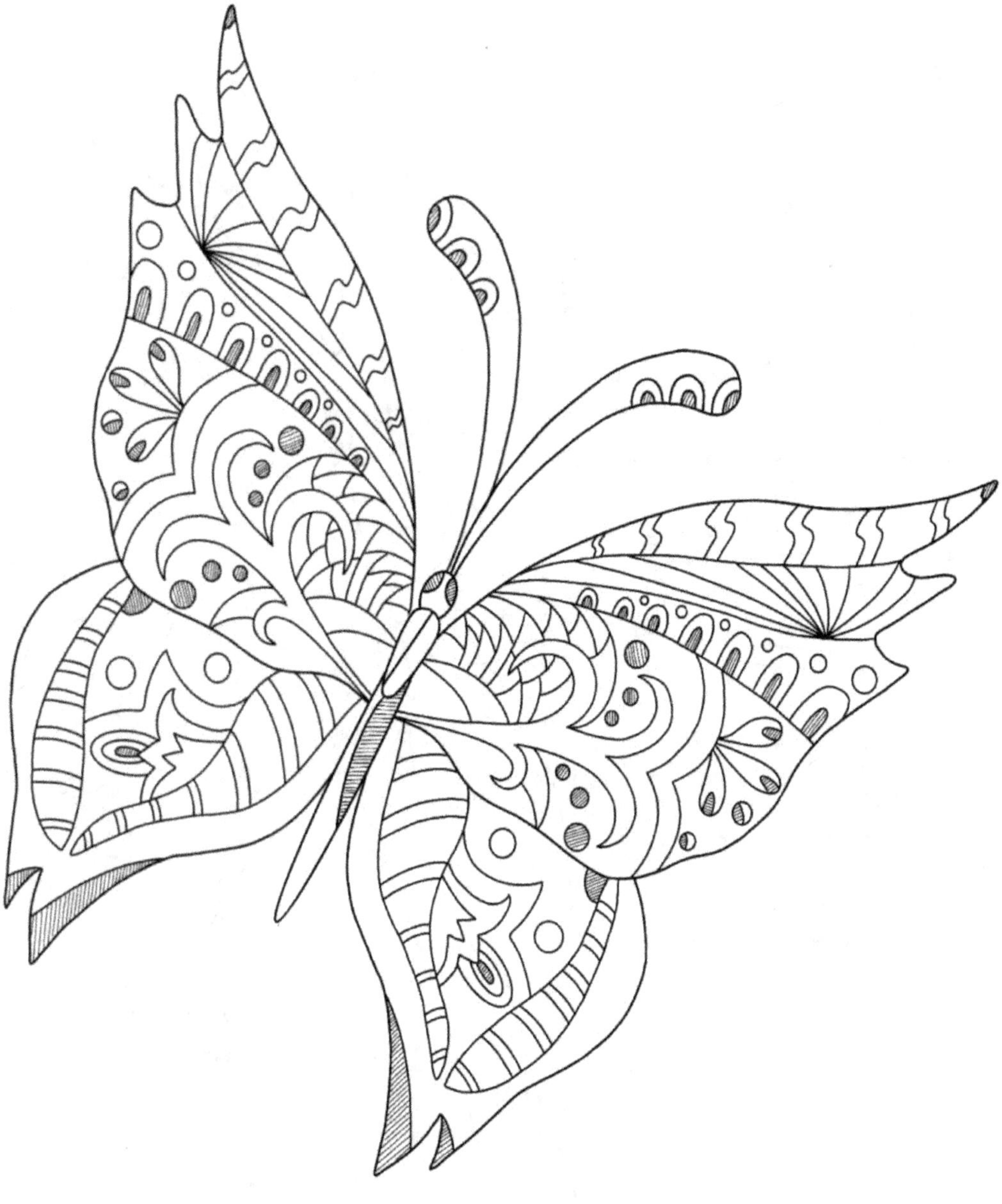
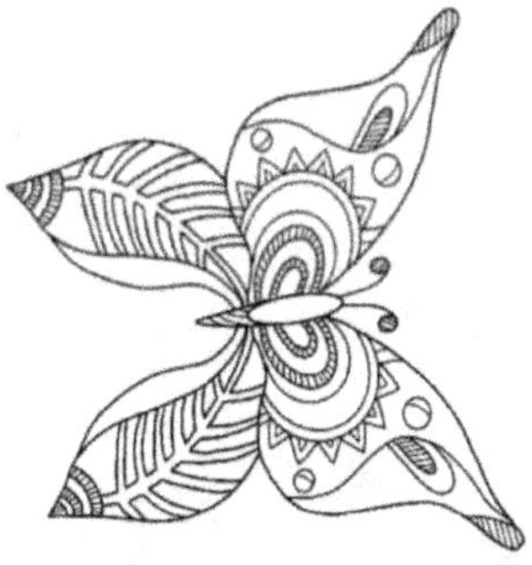

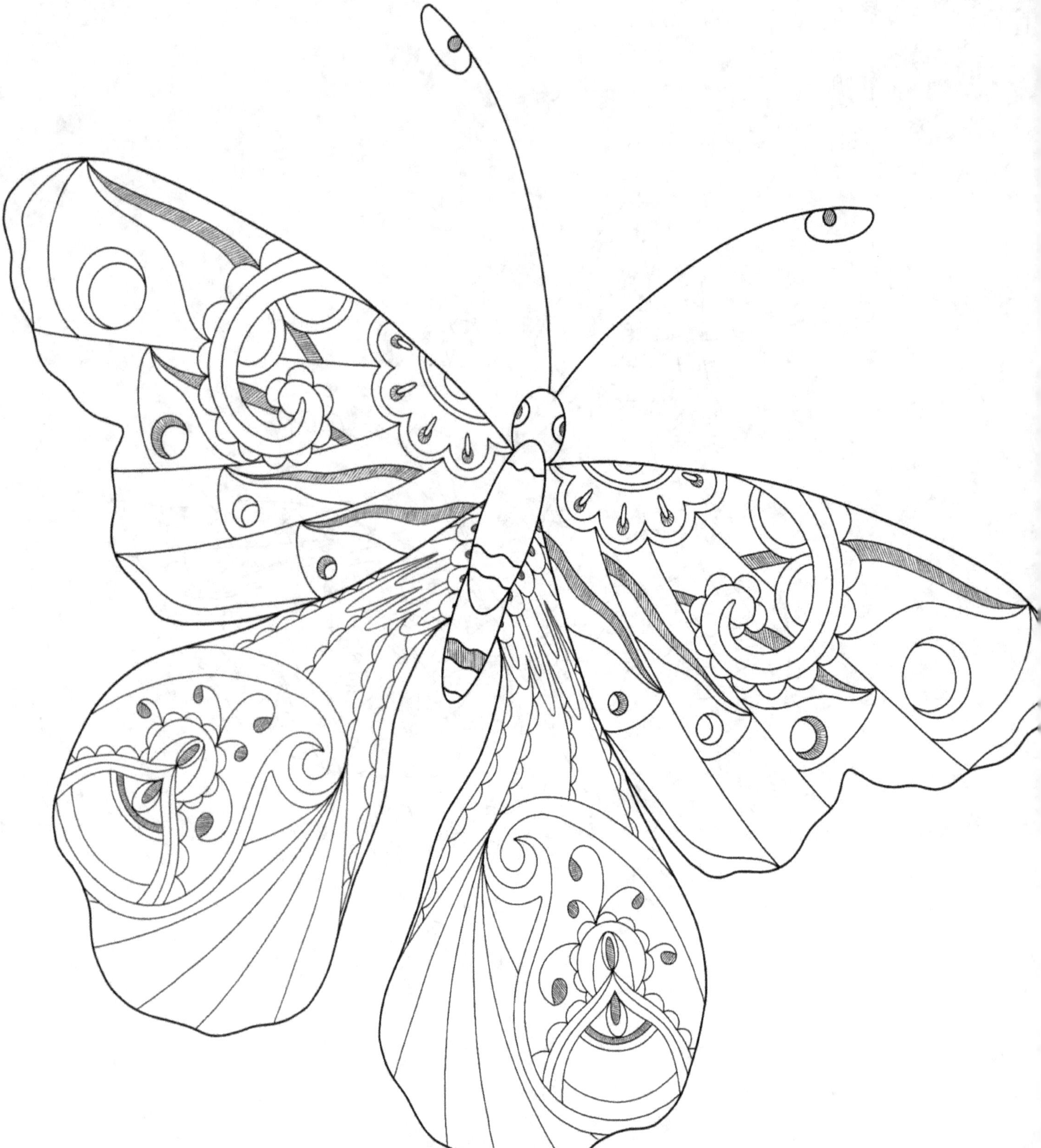

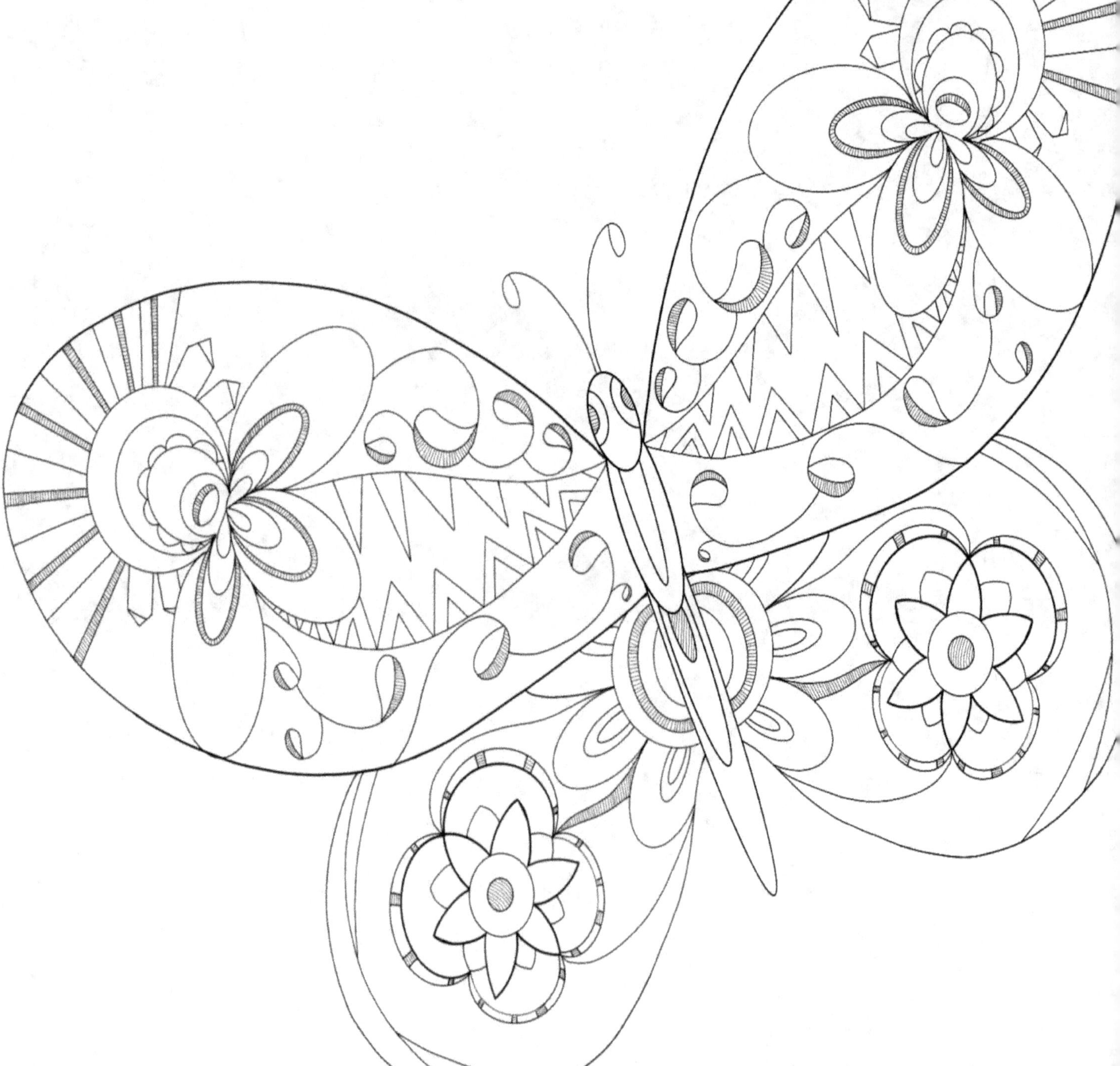

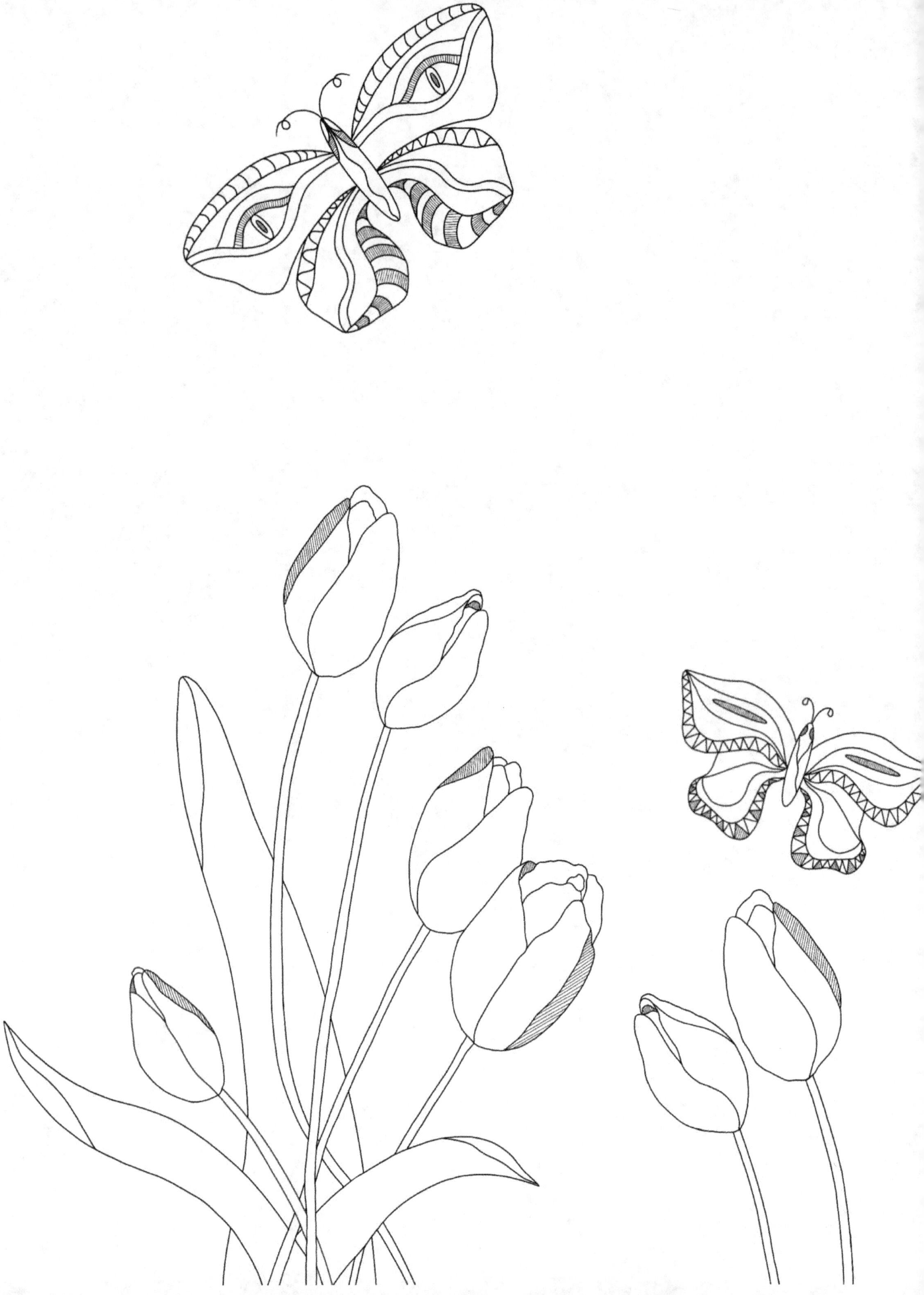

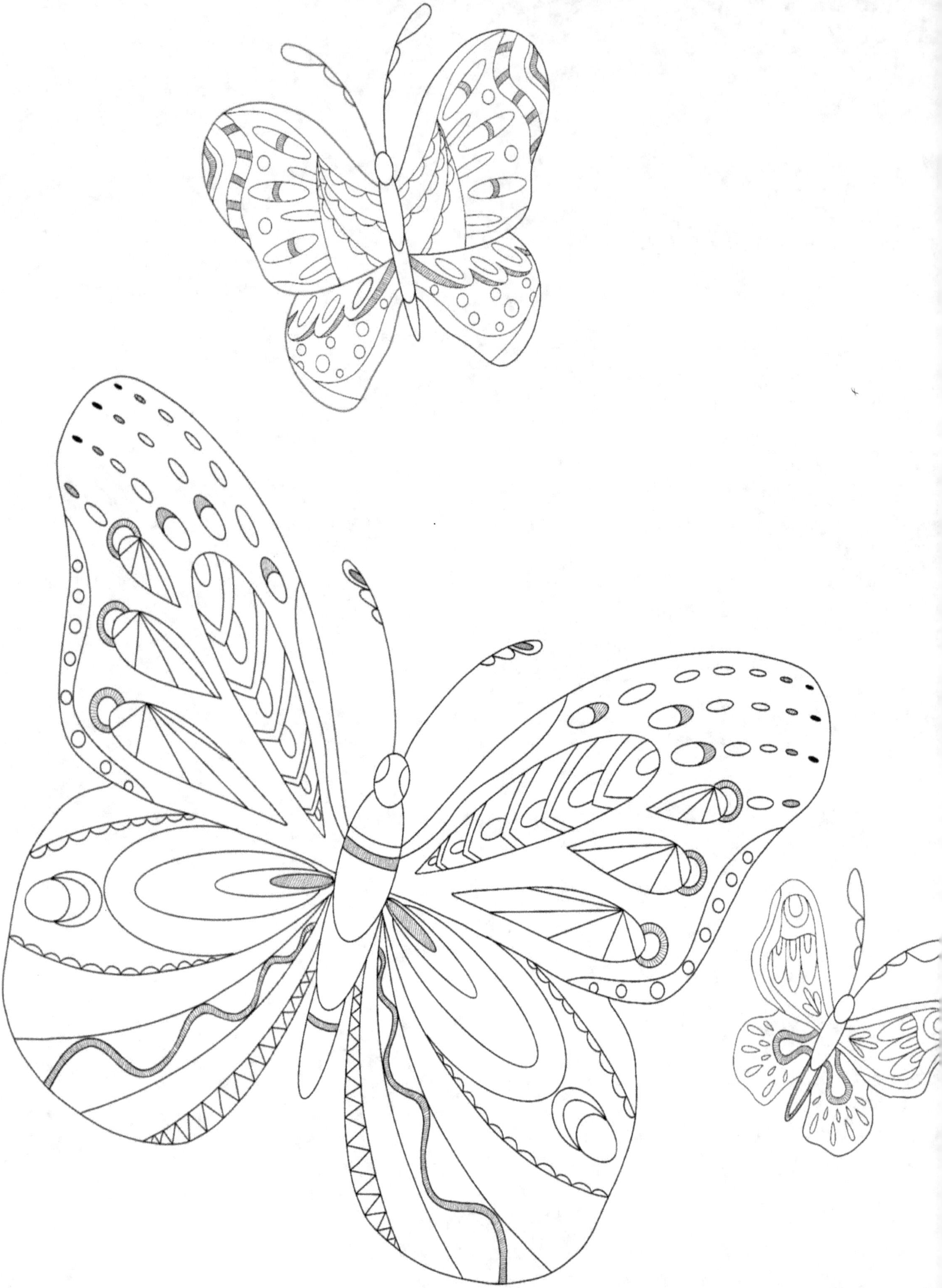

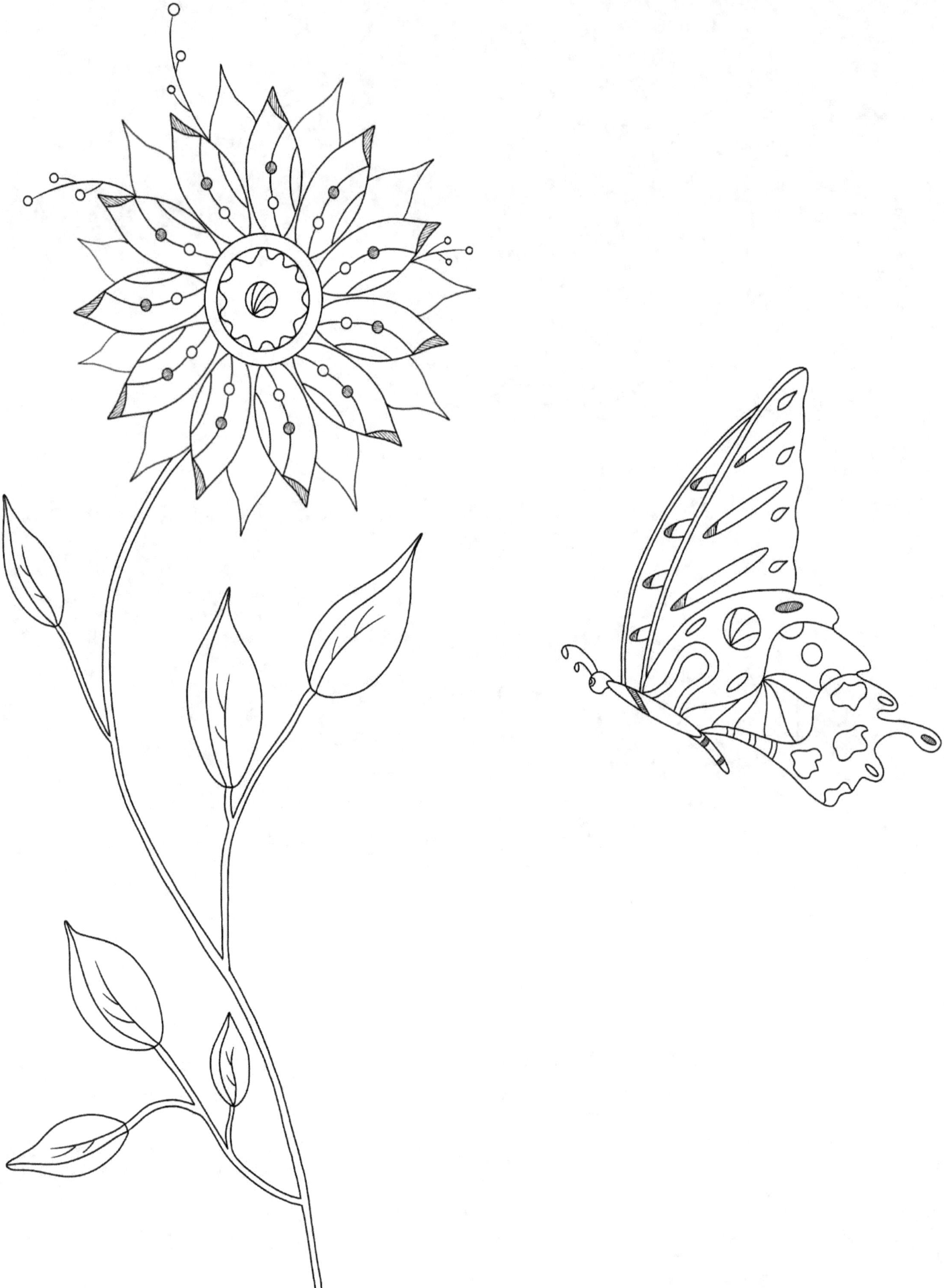

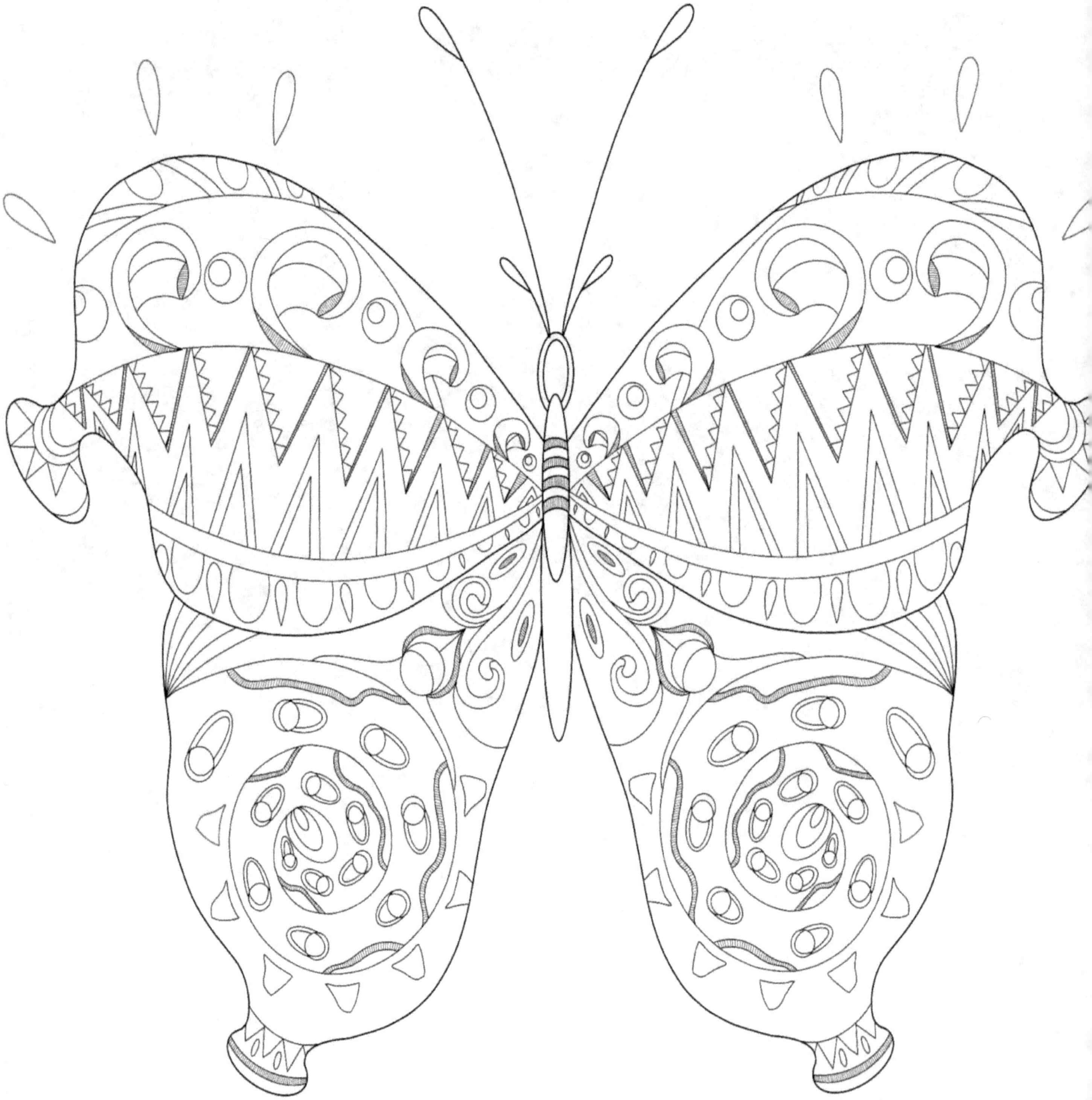

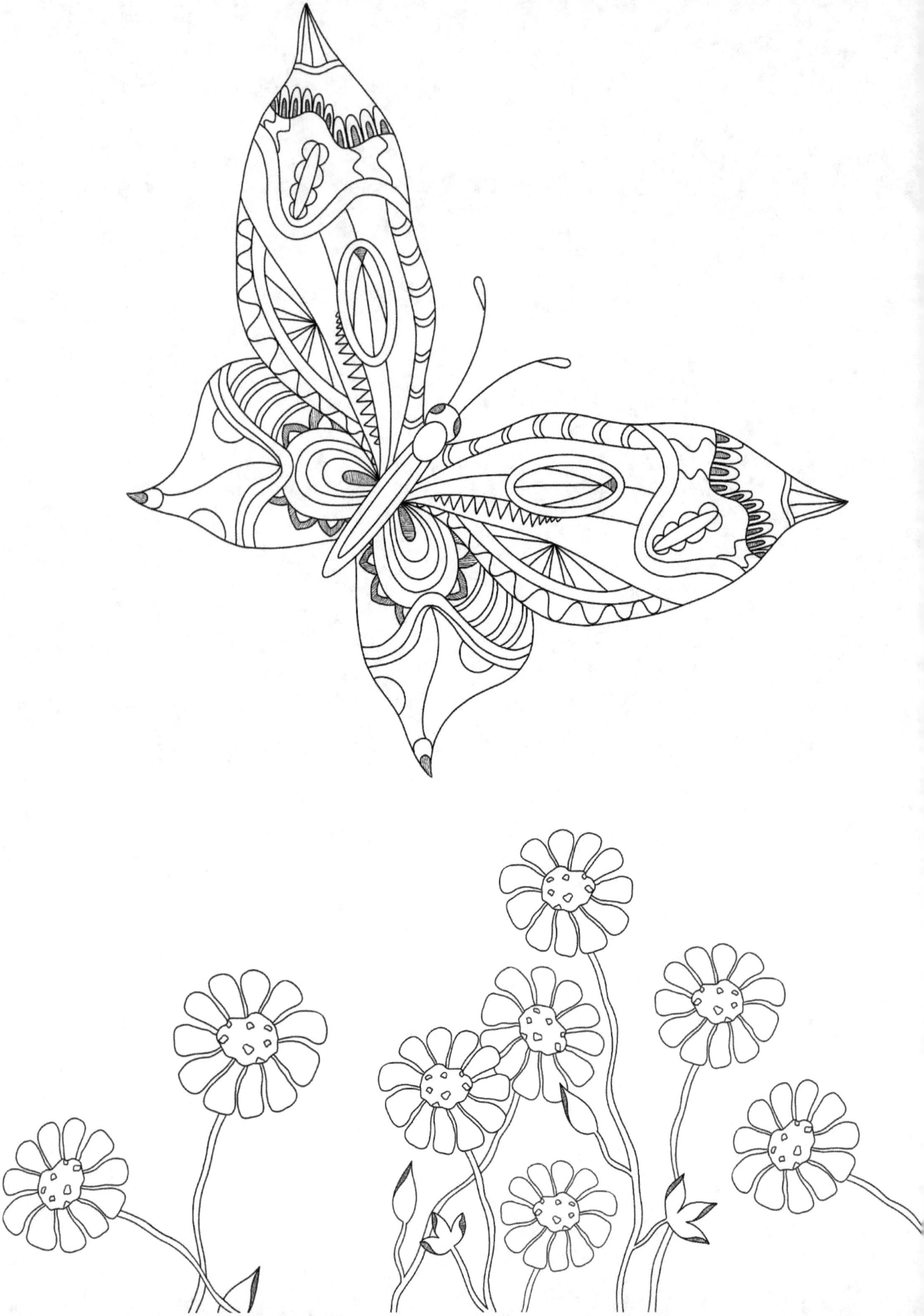

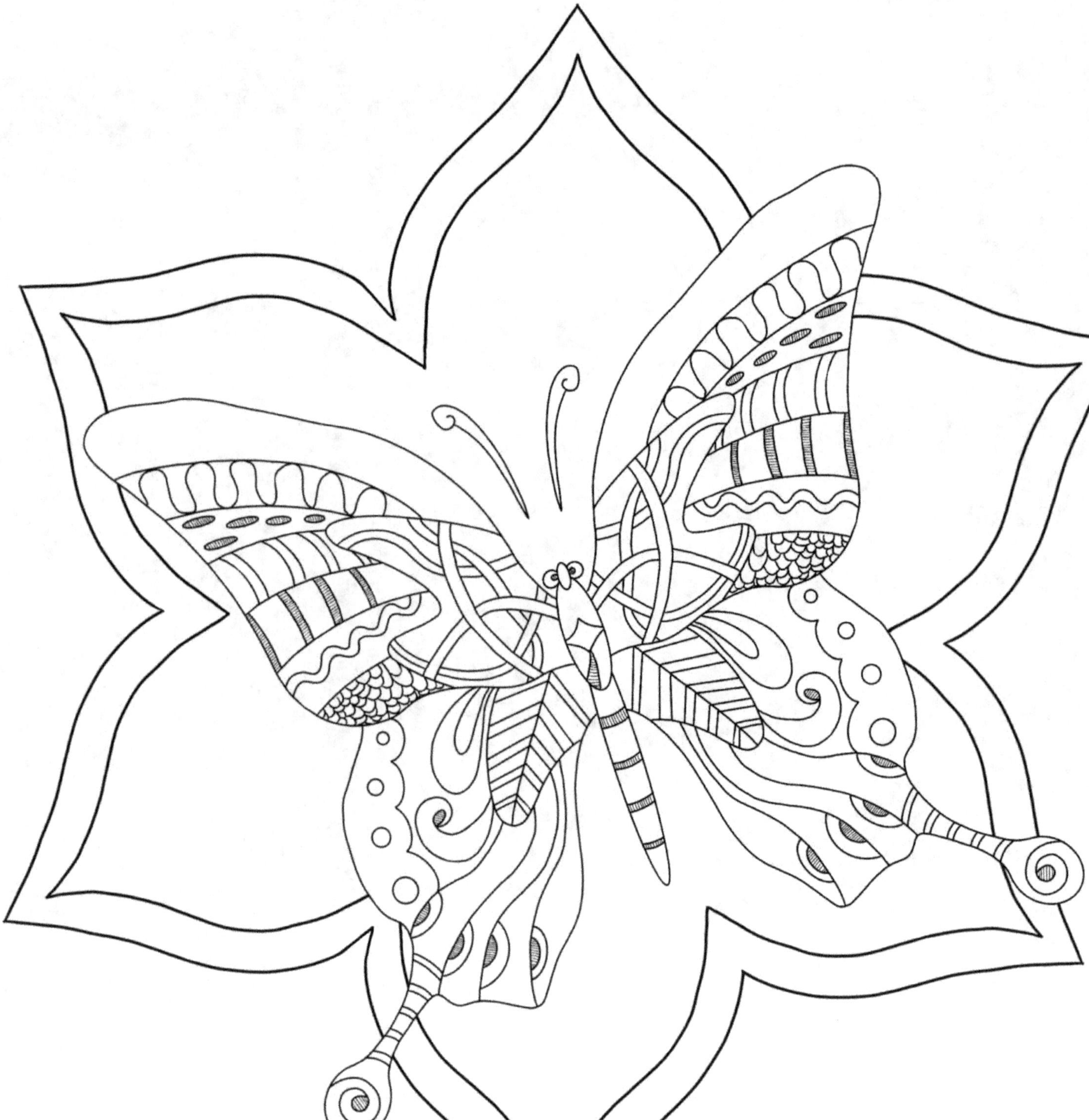

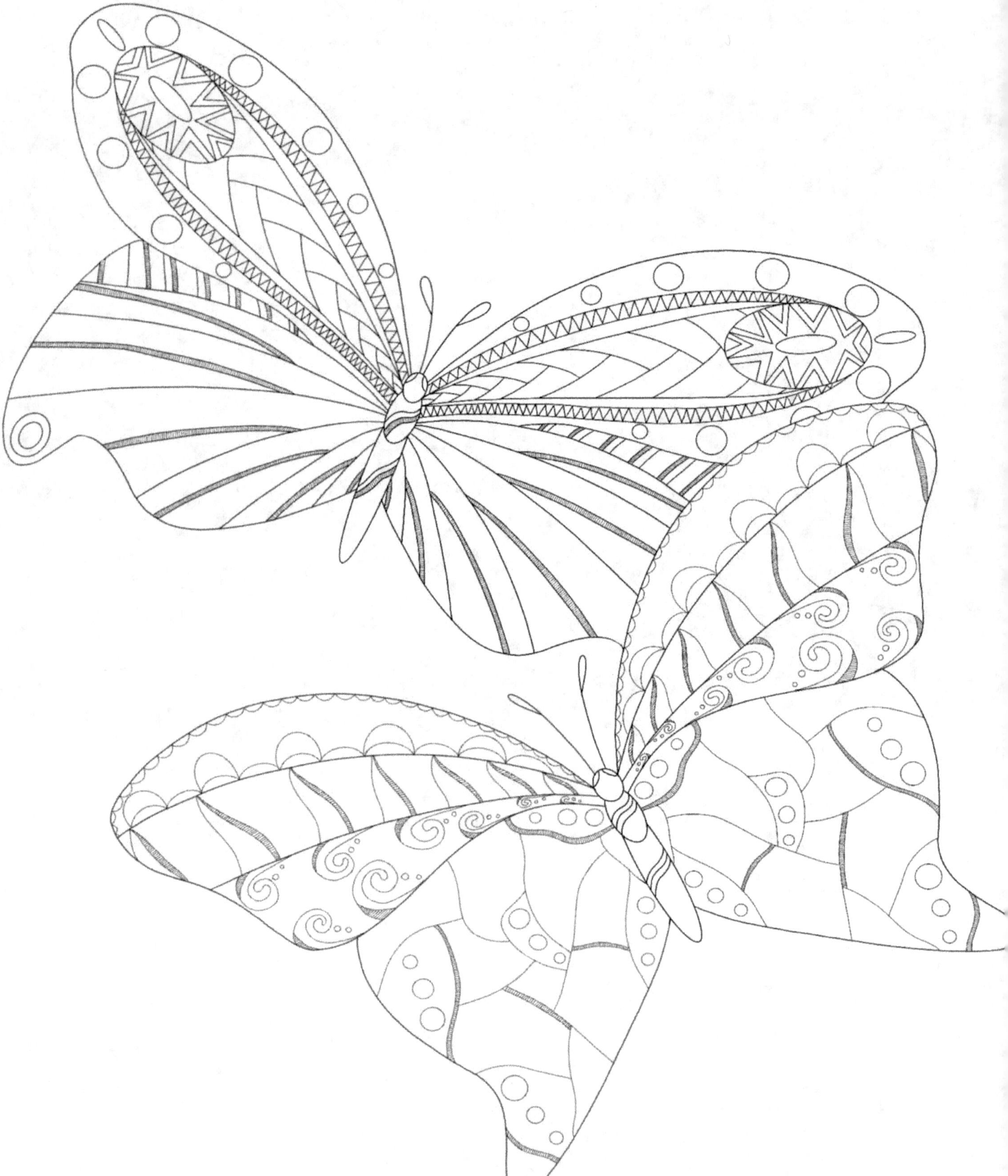

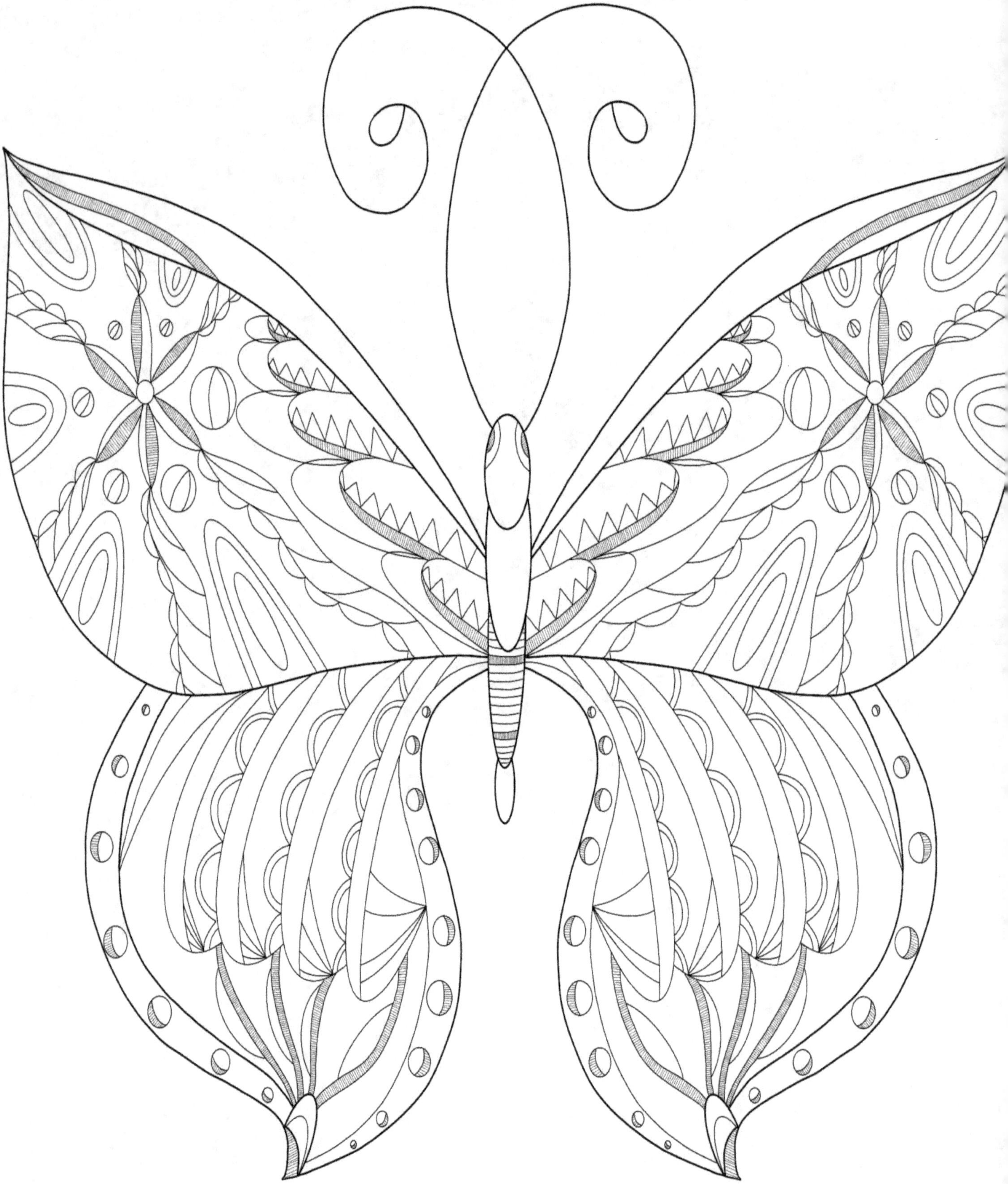

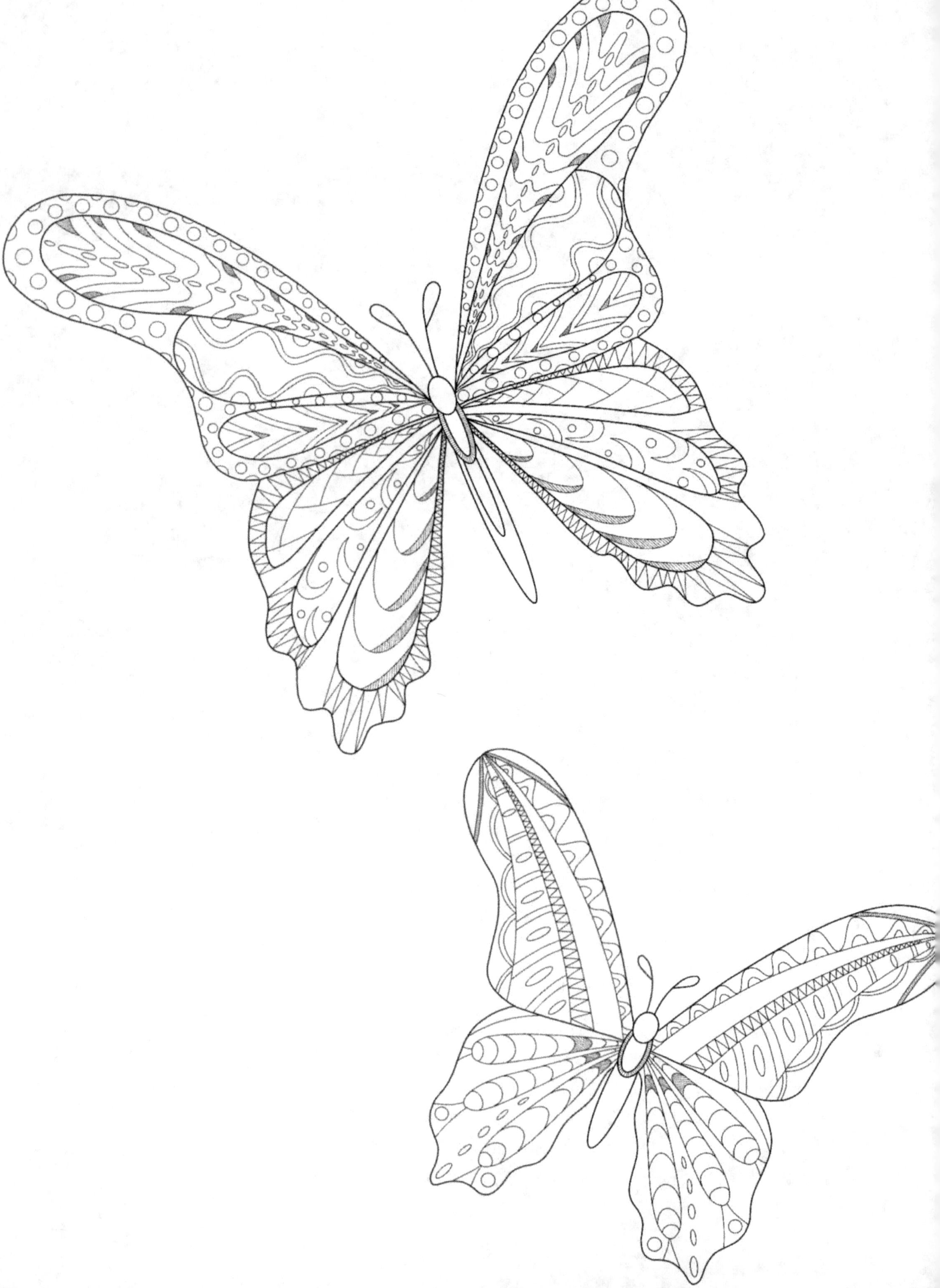

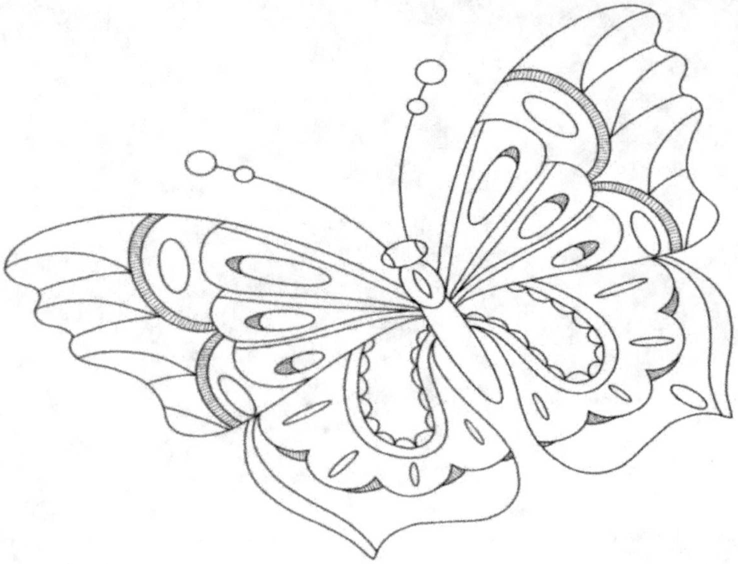

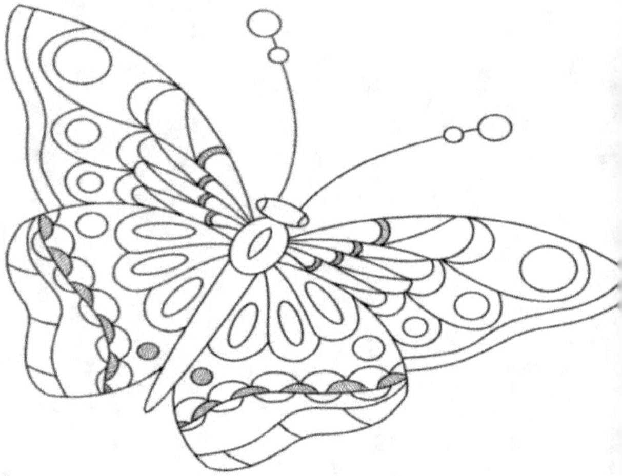

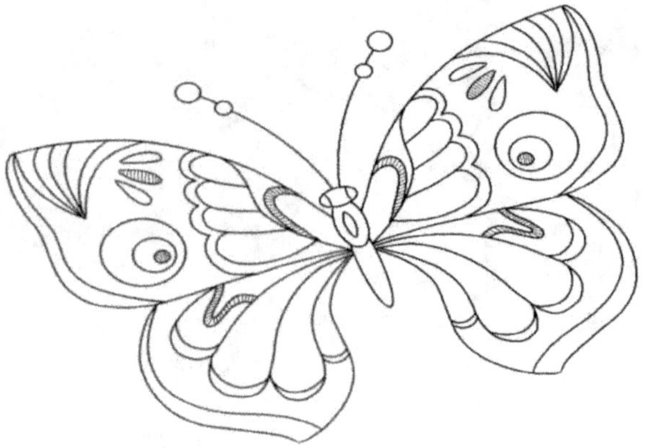

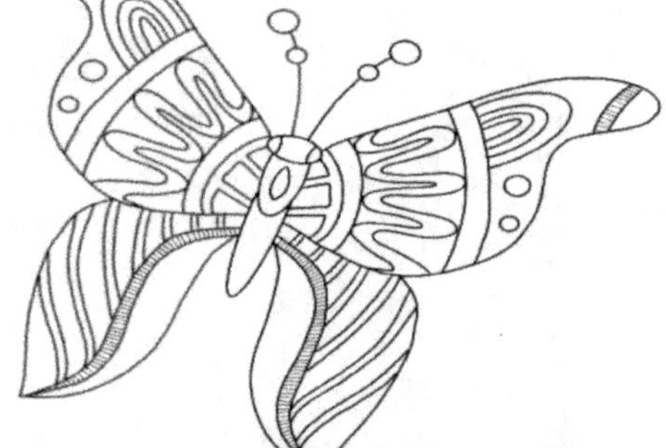

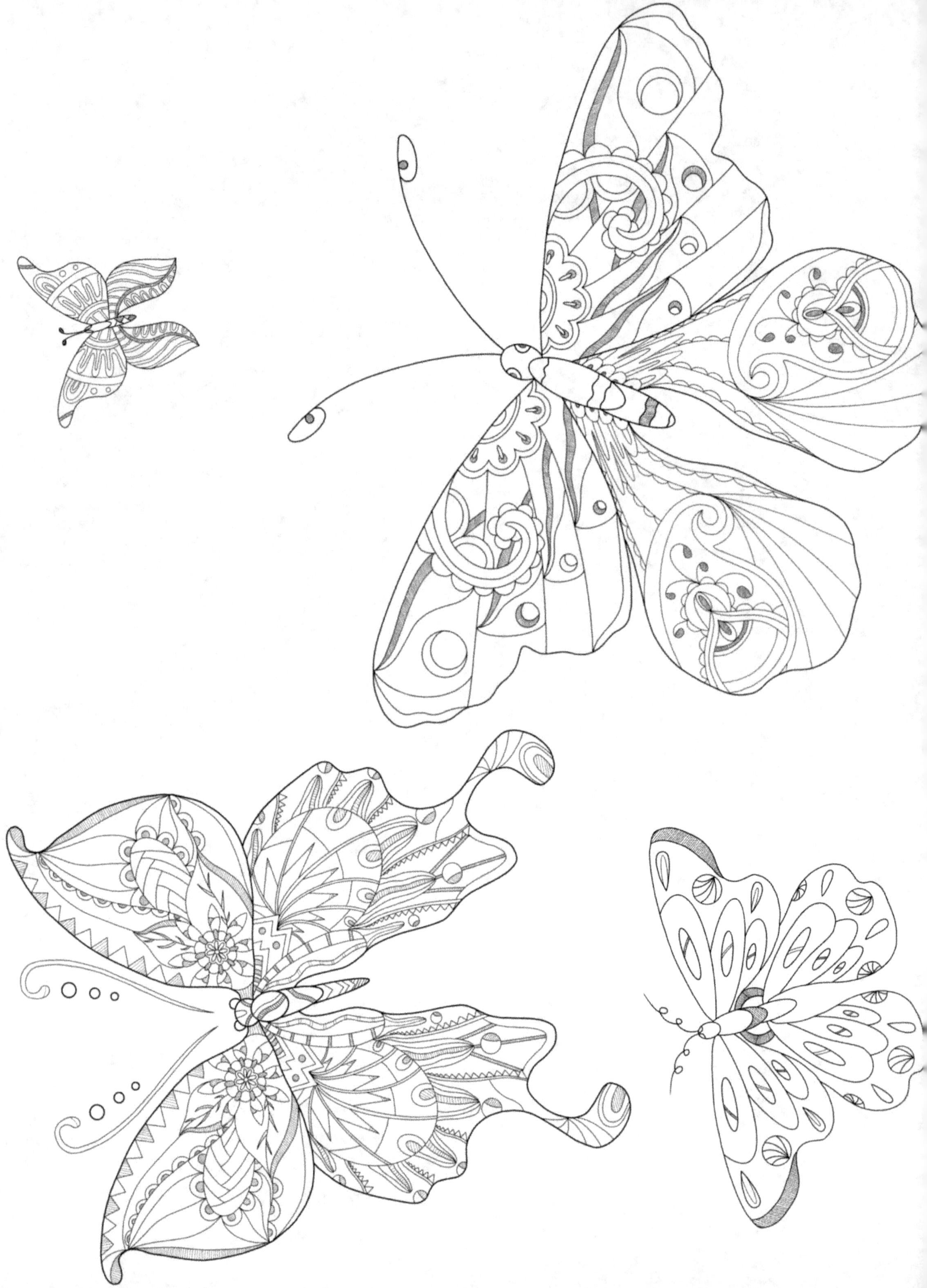

Thank you for purchasing this book.

If you would like to know more about Aryla Publishing Books please visit:-

www.ArylaPublishing.com

Or follow us on
Facebook
Twitter
Instagram
for *free promotions*

@arylapublishing

We would love to know what you think of this book so please leave us a review.

Have a wonderful day ☺

Other Coloring Books from Aryla Publishing

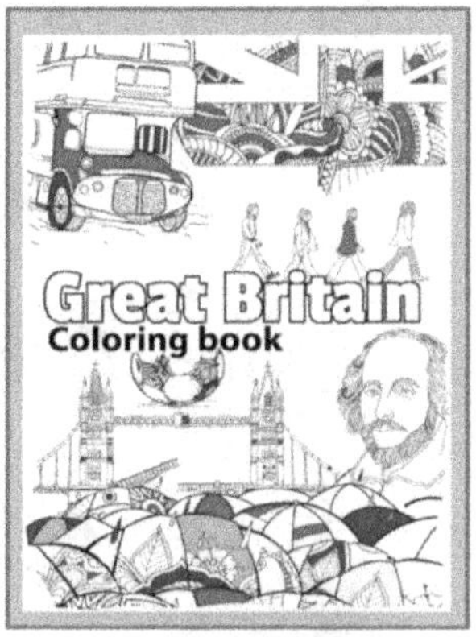

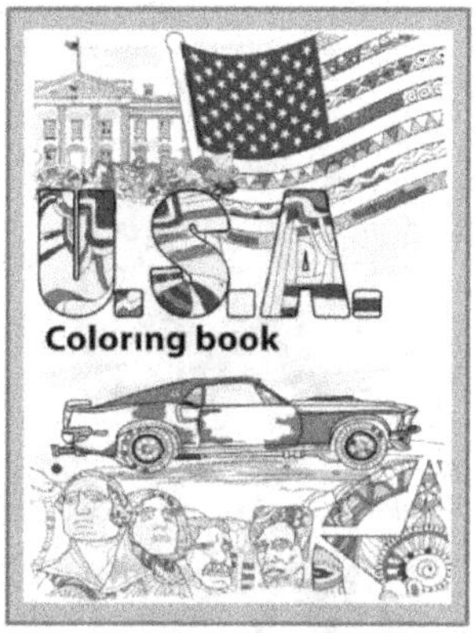

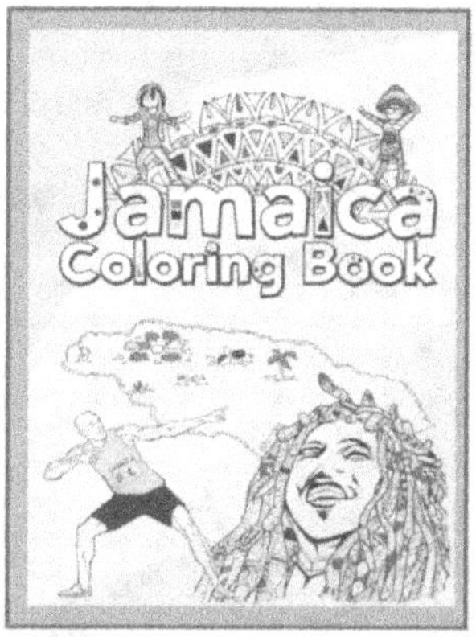

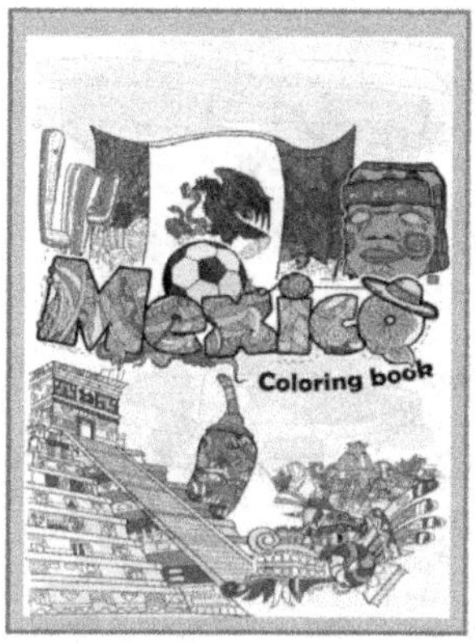

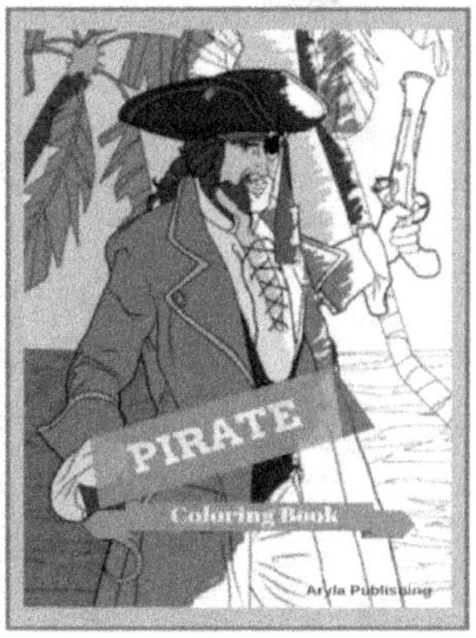

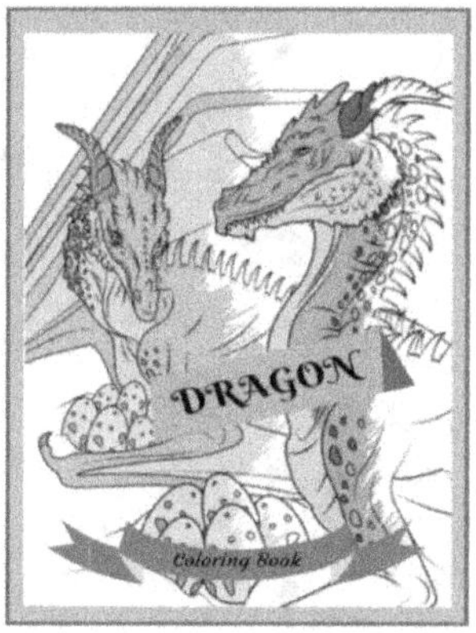

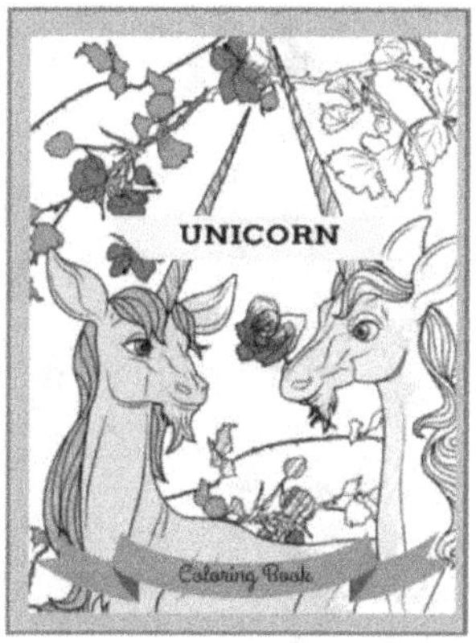

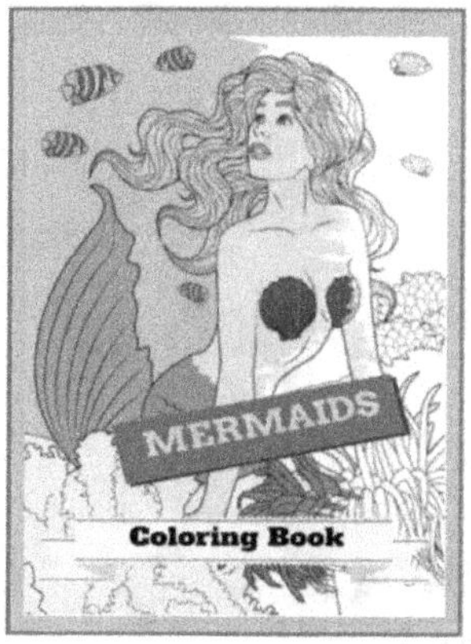

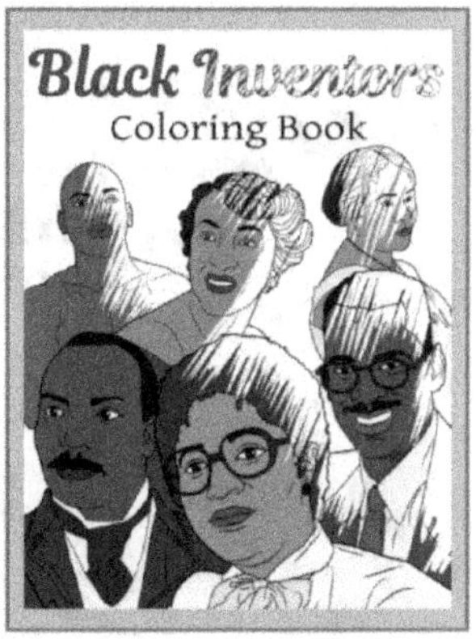

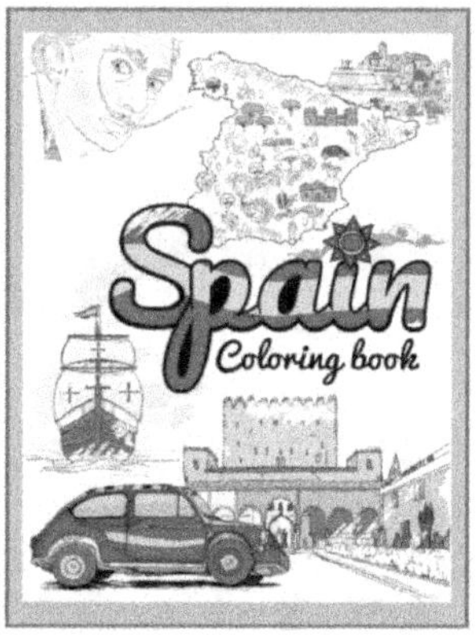

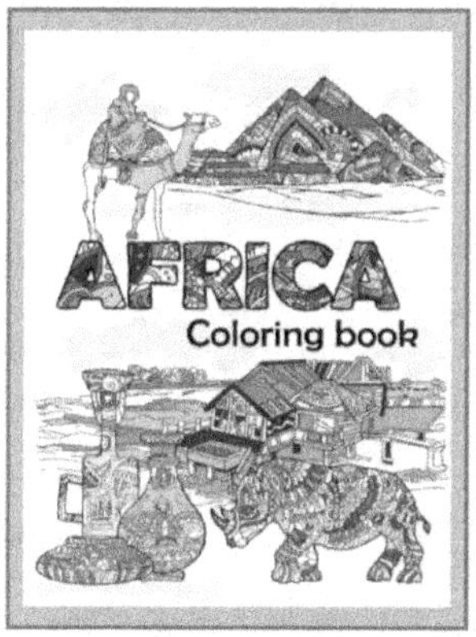

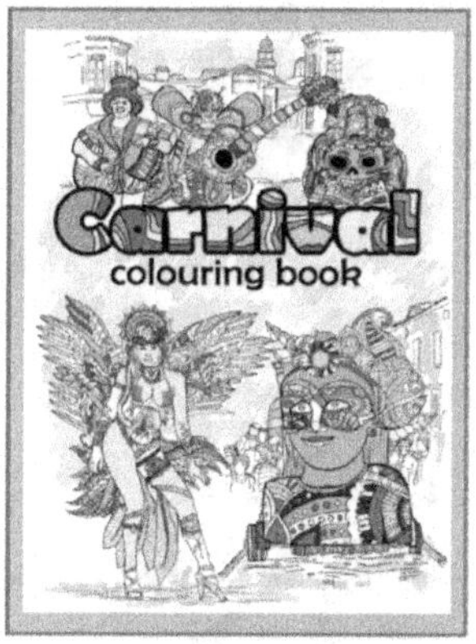

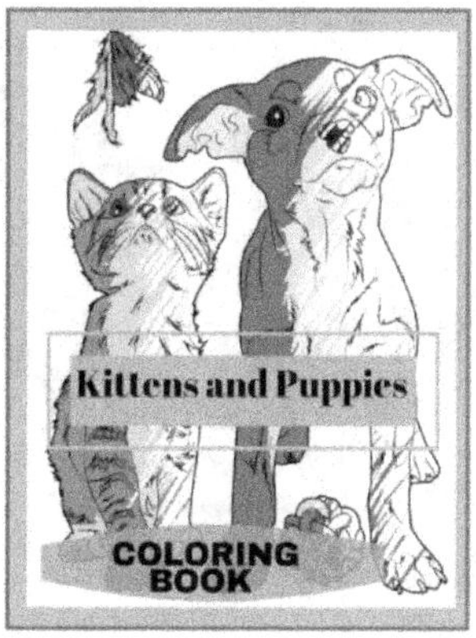

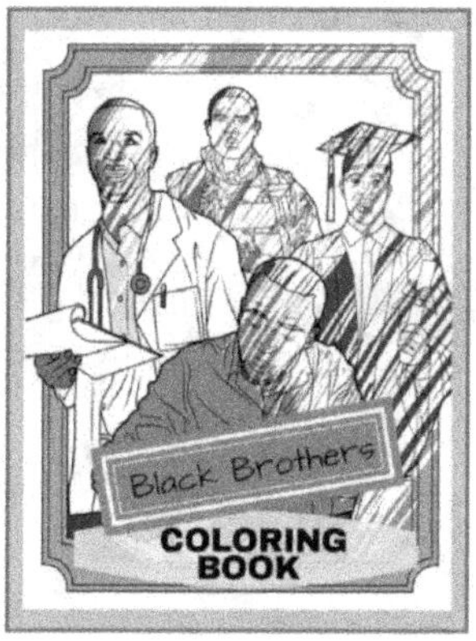

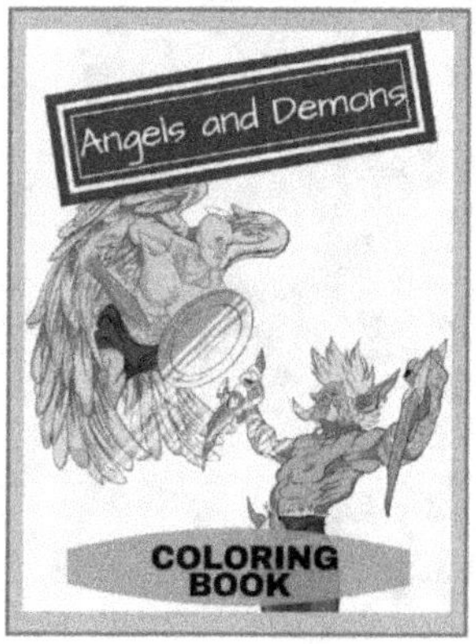

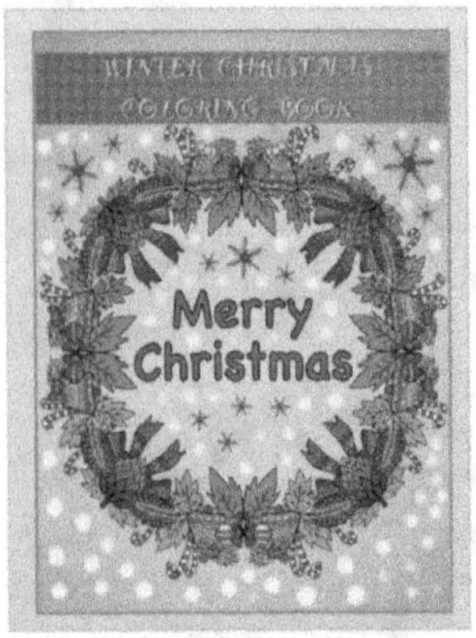
WINTER CHRISTMAS
COLORING BOOK
Merry Christmas
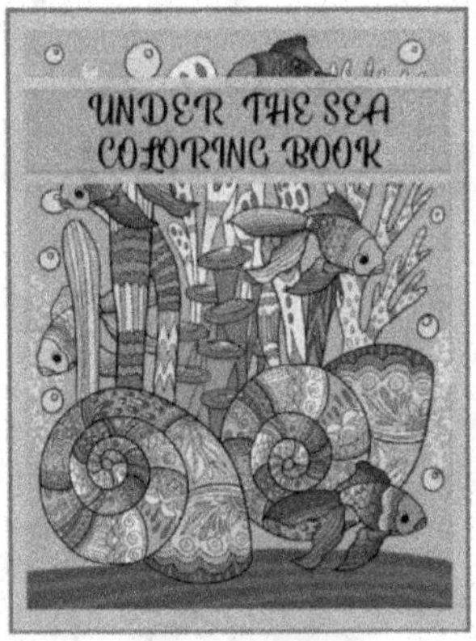
UNDER THE SEA
COLORING BOOK
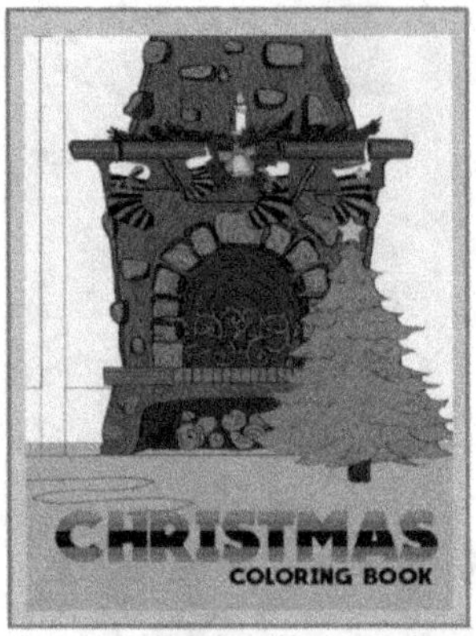
CHRISTMAS
COLORING BOOK
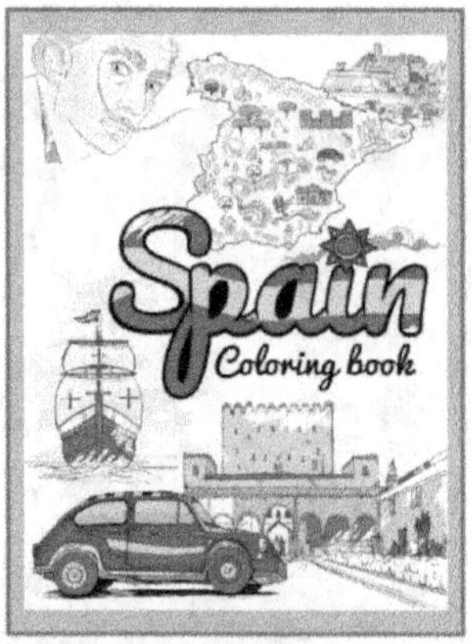
Spain
Coloring book
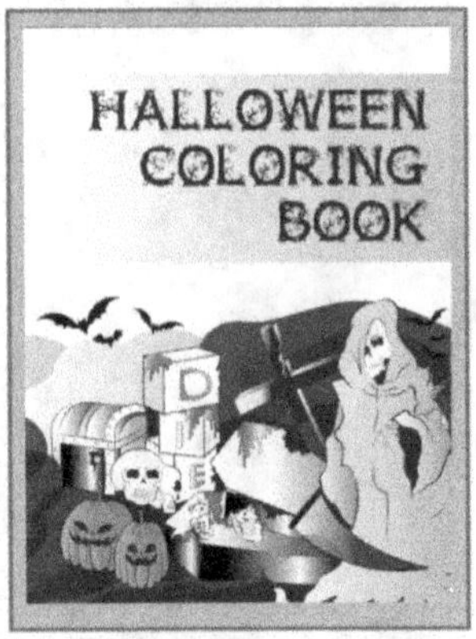
HALLOWEEN
COLORING
BOOK
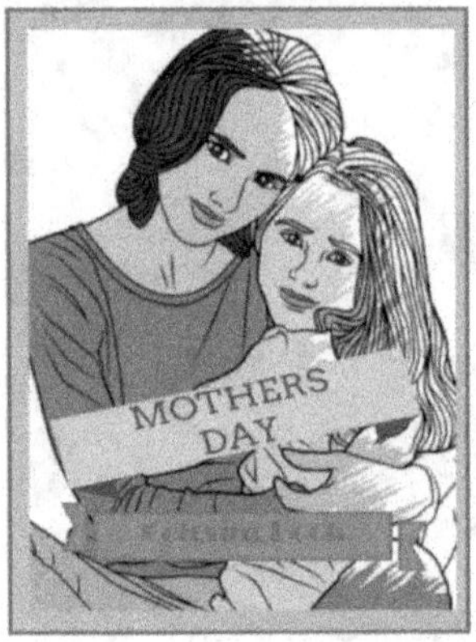
MOTHERS
DAY
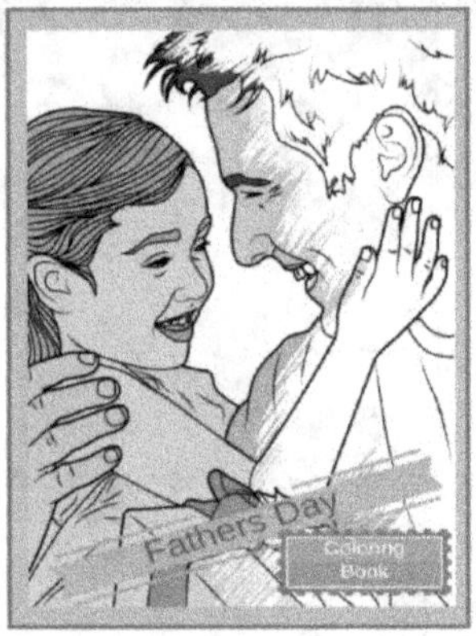
Fathers Day
Coloring
Book
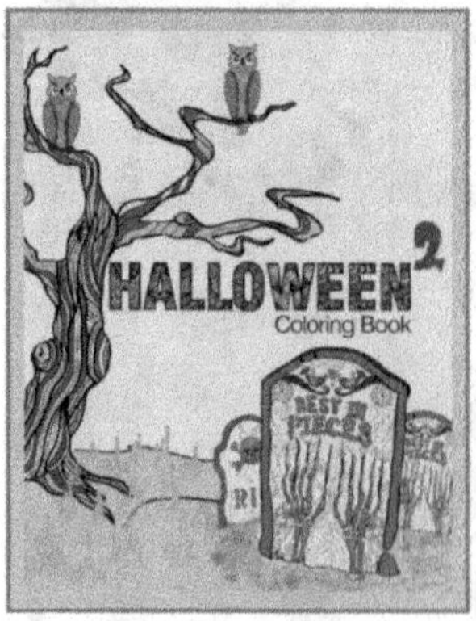
HALLOWEEN 2
Coloring Book
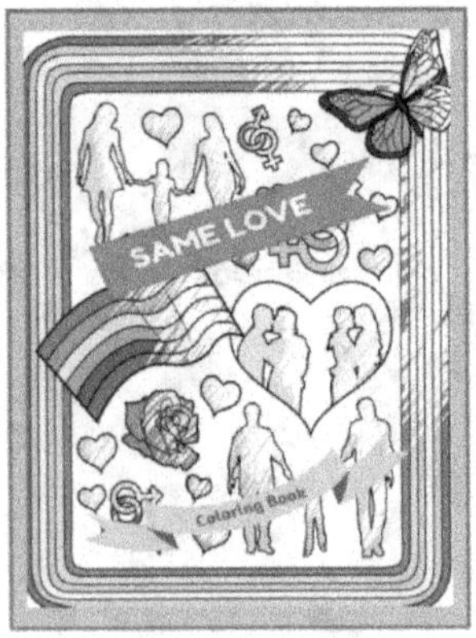
SAME LOVE
Coloring Book
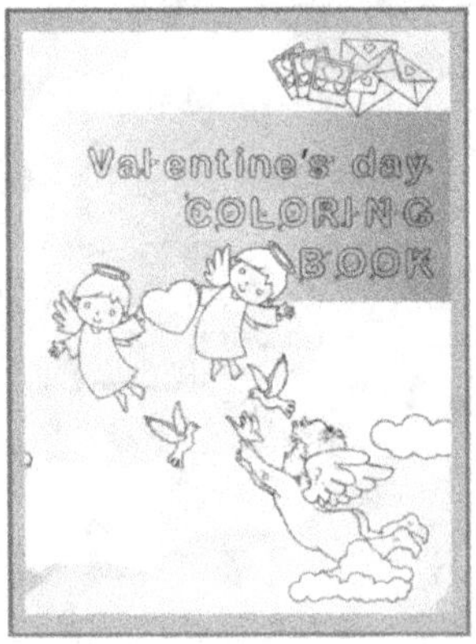
Valentine's day
COLORING
BOOK
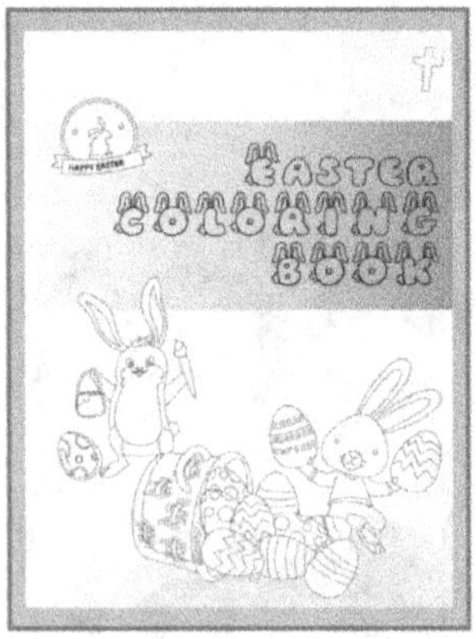
EASTER
COLORING
BOOK
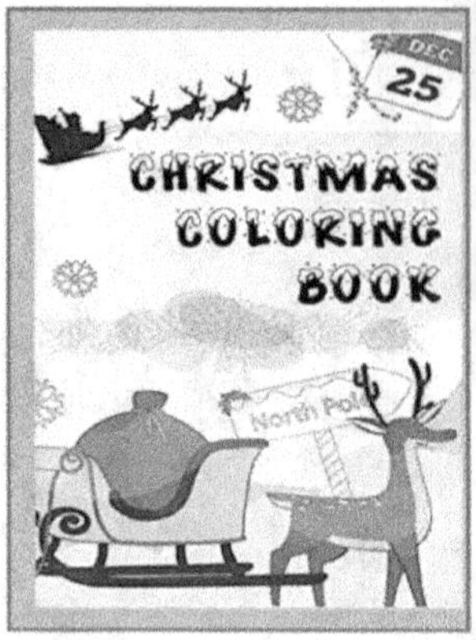
DEC
25
CHRISTMAS
COLORING
BOOK
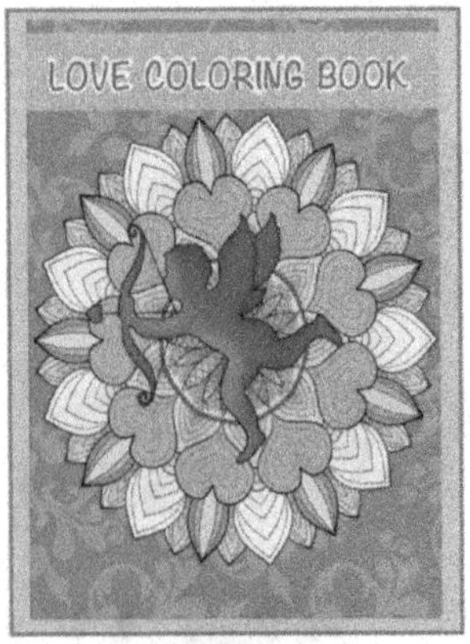
LOVE COLORING BOOK
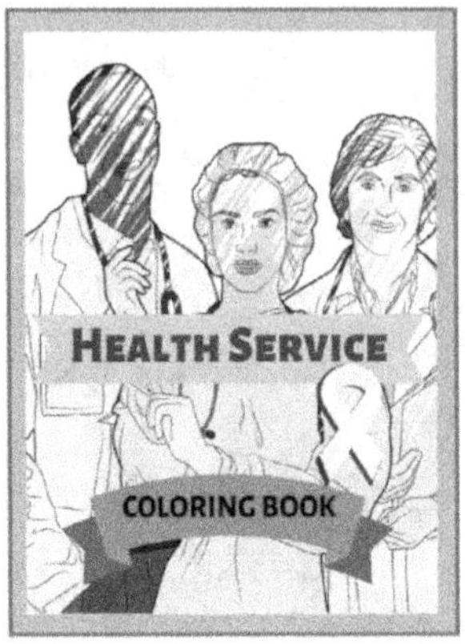
HEALTH SERVICE
COLORING BOOK
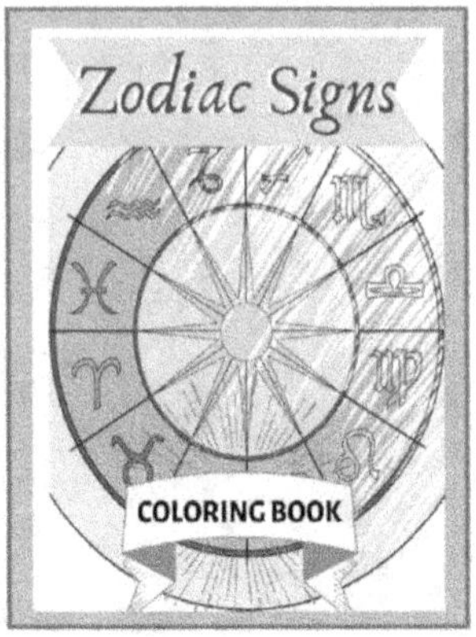
Zodiac Signs
COLORING BOOK
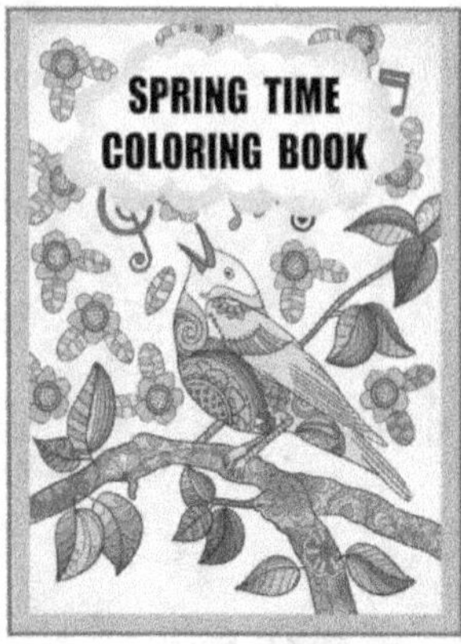
SPRING TIME
COLORING BOOK

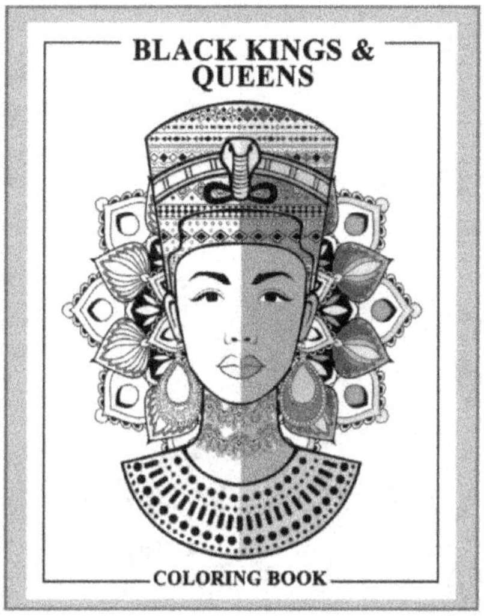
BLACK KINGS &
QUEENS
COLORING BOOK

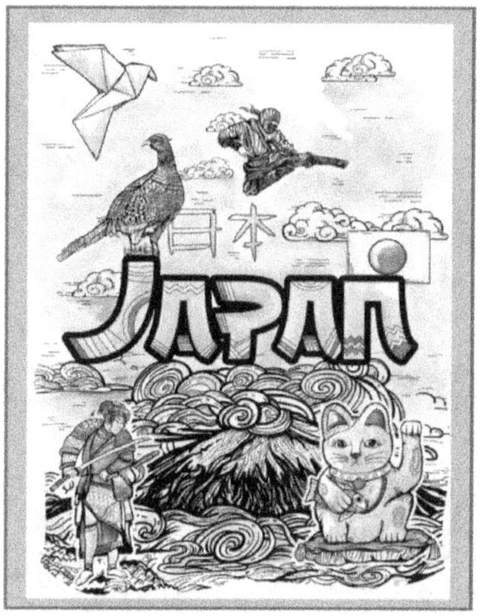
日本
JAPAN

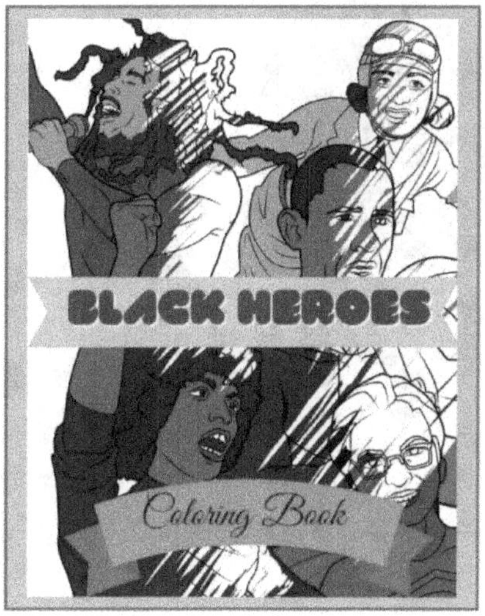
BLACK HEROES
Coloring Book

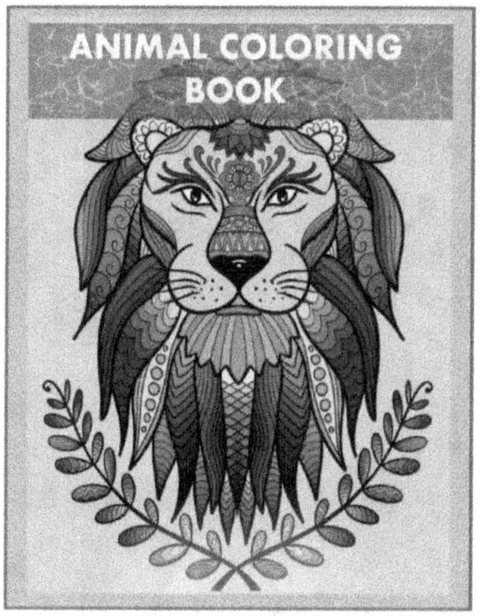
ANIMAL COLORING
BOOK

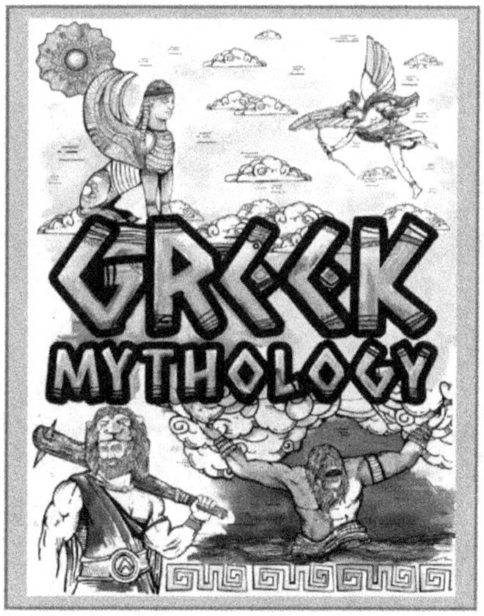
GREEK
MYTHOLOGY

Color In Fun Kids Books

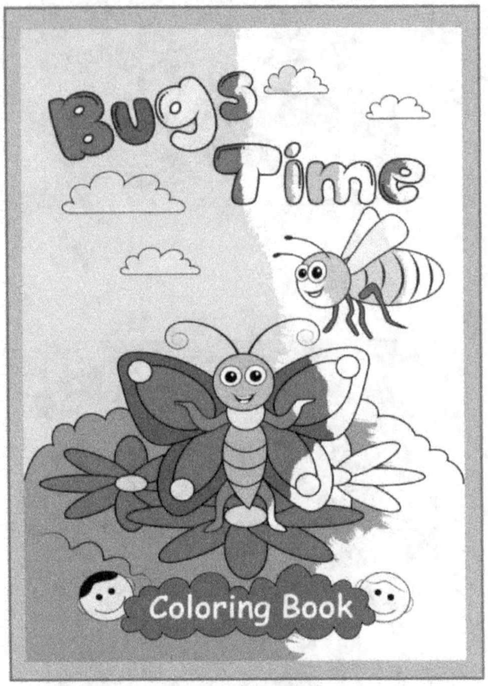

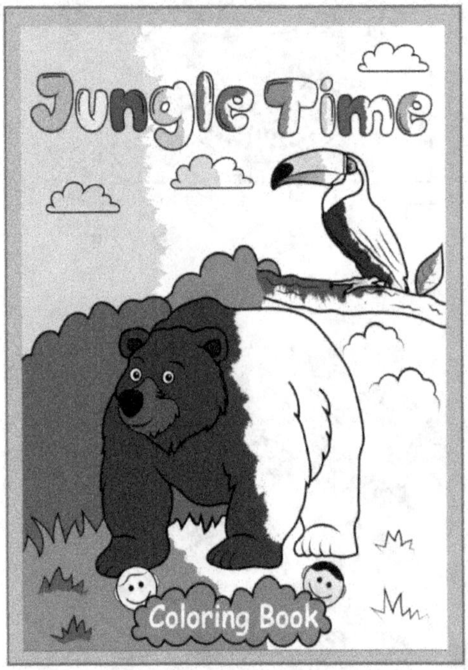

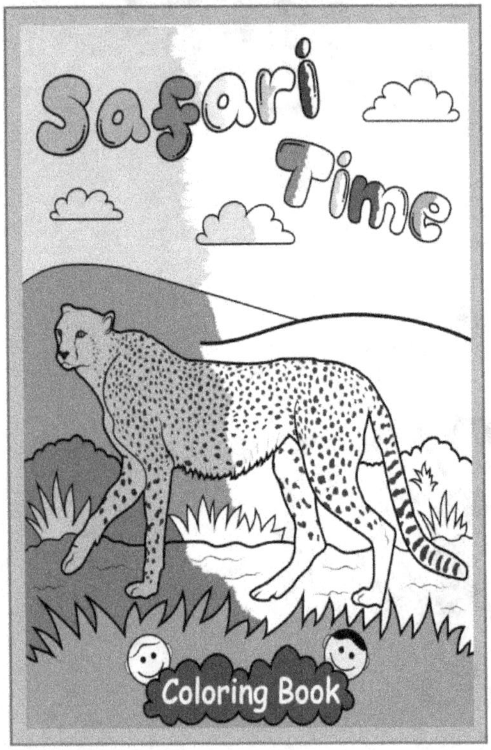

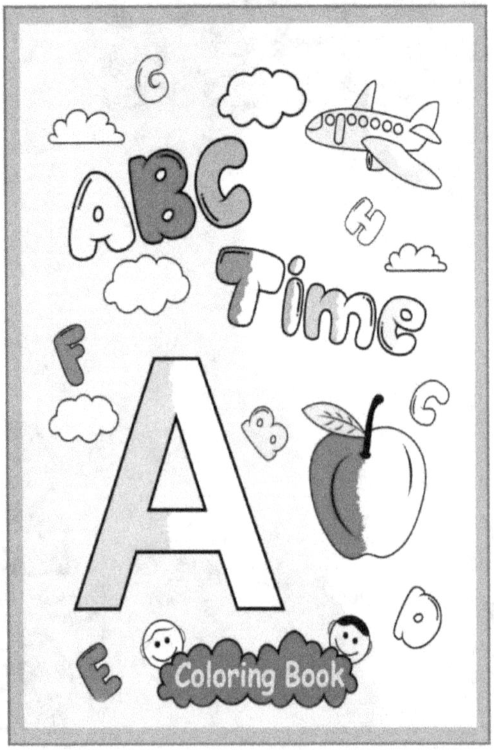

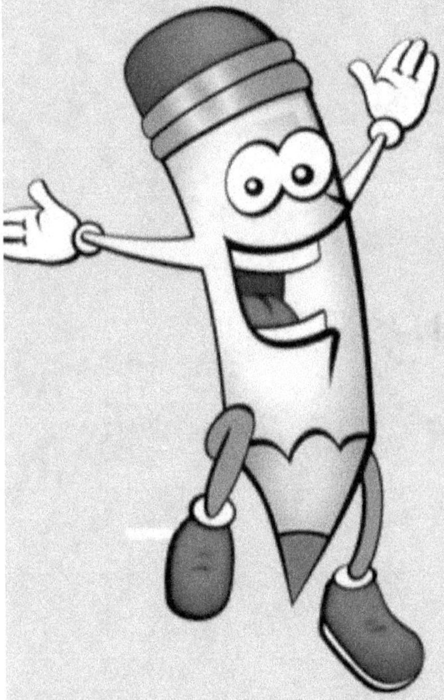

WE WOULD LOVE YOUR FEEDBACK

PLEASE LEAVE REVIEW AT:-

www.ingramcontent.com/pod-product-compliance
Lightning Source LLC
Chambersburg PA
CBHW081747220526
45468CB00008B/2280
9781912675814